Get to Know the USA Vol.1

Enjoy Your Visit

by Motoko Kuroda

Level 4
(2000-word)

IBC パブリッシング

はじめに

　ラダーシリーズは、「はしご (ladder)」を使って一歩一歩上を目指すように、学習者の実力に合わせ、無理なくステップアップできるよう開発された英文リーダーのシリーズです。

　リーディング力をつけるためには、繰り返したくさん読むこと、いわゆる「多読」がもっとも効果的な学習法であると言われています。多読では、「1. 速く 2. 訳さず英語のまま 3. なるべく辞書を使わず」に読むことが大切です。スピードを計るなど、速く読むよう心がけましょう（たとえば TOEIC® テストの音声スピードはおよそ 1 分間に 150 語です）。そして 1 語ずつ訳すのではなく、英語を英語のまま理解するくせをつけるようにします。こうして読み続けるうちに語感がついてきて、だんだんと英語が理解できるようになるのです。まずは、ラダーシリーズの中からあなたのレベルに合った本を選び、少しずつ英文に慣れ親しんでください。たくさんの本を手にとるうちに、英文書がすらすら読めるようになってくるはずです。

《本シリーズの特徴》

- 中学校レベルから中級者レベルまで5段階に分かれています。自分に合ったレベルからスタートしてください。
- クラシックから現代文学、ノンフィクション、ビジネスと幅広いジャンルを扱っています。あなたの興味に合わせてタイトルを選べます。
- 巻末のワードリストで、いつでもどこでも単語の意味を確認できます。レベル1、2では、文中の全ての単語が、レベル3以上は中学校レベル外の単語が掲載されています。
- カバーにヘッドホーンマークのついているタイトルは、オーディオ・サポートがあります。ウェブから購入／ダウンロードし、リスニング教材としても併用できます。

《使用語彙について》

レベル1：中学校で学習する単語約1000語

レベル2：レベル1の単語＋使用頻度の高い単語約300語

レベル3：レベル1の単語＋使用頻度の高い単語約600語

レベル4：レベル1の単語＋使用頻度の高い単語約1000語

レベル5：語彙制限なし

CONTENTS

Part 1

1. Pieces of a puzzle
   —a look across the States 3

2. A land with an attitude
   —getting a feel for the national spirit 12

3. Give me a break!—the national holidays 23

4. All shapes, colors and sizes
   —the American people 32

Part 2

5. Reach out and touch someone
   —communicating in the U.S. 49

6. Getting where you want to go
   —transportation in the U.S. 61

7. A place to lay one's head—where to stay 74

8. Chowing down—where the food is 80

9. Big bucks, little bucks
   —where to spend your money 92

10. Getting in on the action—sports and the arts .. 105

11. Money makes the world go round 115

    About the Author 121

    Word List 124

Part 1

Part 1 covers general information and American culture. Knowing the background of the country and its people helps one better understand what one sees today.

読みはじめる前に

パート1で使われている用語です。わからない語は巻末のワードリストで確認しましょう。

- [ ] immigration
- [ ] individual
- [ ] suburb
- [ ] equator
- [ ] legal
- [ ] sales tax
- [ ] affordable
- [ ] opportunity
- [ ] will
- [ ] freedom
- [ ] religion
- [ ] small talk
- [ ] responsibility
- [ ] Celsius
- [ ] menorah
- [ ] state law / federal law

知っておくと便利なアメリカの知識

time zones 国土の広いアメリカでは、アラスカ、ハワイをのぞいて4つのタイムゾーンを採用している。一番早く朝を迎えるのは、東部地区(Eastern)で、山地(Mountain)、中部(Central)、太平洋(Pacific)と西に向かうにつれ1時間ごと遅れて朝を迎える。

Red America/Blue America Red Americaとは、共和党を支持する主に米中部に位置する州(31州)を指し、Blue Americaは東海岸、西海岸の大都市を抱える州を中心にした民主党支持の州(19州)を指す。

"racial melting pot" vs "mixed salad" アメリカの移民社会を、「人種のメルティング・ポット」と表すのはよく知られているが、最近では、「ミックスド・サラダ」という表現が使われるようになってきた。ポットの中で煮込んでしまい、全体が渾然一体になるイメージより、サラダのように素材の持ち味は残したまま、混ざり合っているというところから、主流に組み込まれないで、バックグランドを大切にしようという民主主義的な動きが強くなっていることの現れとみることができる。

1. Pieces of a puzzle
—a look across the States

It's a "supersize" country

America is huge. Everyone knows that. However, many people don't really understand what all that means. The United States of America is a supersize country in many ways.

First, it is huge as far as land mass. It is so big there are four different time zones. When it is 9 a.m. in New York it is still only 6 a.m. in Los Angeles. A trip by plane from coast to coast will take six hours. To fly from New York to Alaska or Hawaii will take much longer.

Because of its size, the United States has many different climates. These differences in nature also affect the way people live, what they value and how they feel about things.

Second, everything is spread out across the country. Local governments have the power to make legal decisions on many issues. It is surprising to learn that so many things are covered by state laws instead of national, or federal laws. Also, laws do not stop at the state level. Cities and towns also have their own laws. For example, you can find a "dry town," that is, one that greatly limits the sale of alcohol, within a larger area that does not limit alcohol so much.

School systems, too, are different from district to district. What is taught in schools can also be very different from school to school. Also, the school system itself can vary widely. In some areas, for example, middle school can be made up of sixth grade to eighth grade. In other areas, it can be from fifth grade to eighth grade.

The economically powerful areas are also more spread across the United States than they are in Japan. The headquarters of major companies are not always to be found in the big cities, such as New York, Washington, D.C., or Los Angeles. Headquarters could be in Texas, or Ohio, or anywhere. This also affects people's ways of life, values, and attitudes in different areas.

I can talk about the way people live and their attitudes in cities such as New York, for example, but the attitudes and lives of people in New York may not be the same as those of people in Florida. It means little to talk about things in a general way about the United States or the American people, as things are different all over.

You may hear or read about "the American lifestyle" on TV and magazines in Japan. Do not take what you hear as general information. It is likely to just be true for one certain area. Just because you hear or read that "it's very popular in America," doesn't mean that it is popular. It's more likely to only be true for a very small group of people in one area. A person living in a college town in California may say "Americans are very easy-going about fashion. It's okay to go anywhere in just a T-shirt and shorts." But, that may not be okay in a college town on the East Coast. It is not okay in New York City. If you really want to know about something in a certain area, the best way is to ask local people from that area.

Big laws, little laws—state versus federal

When you enter the U.S., you have to fill in the immigration papers at the airport. This is a part of immigration law. Immigration law is a national, or federal law, and it may be the only federal law you have to directly deal with while you are in the U.S.

In the U.S., many everyday laws are state laws, not federal laws. How old you have to be to get a driver's license, how much the sales tax is, what you need to get married, what you need to get divorced, and so on. These things are all covered by state laws. A sixteen-year-old teenager can get a driver's license in some states, but has to wait till he is seventeen or eighteen in other states. You may have to pay sales tax on clothes in New York, but not on clothes in Connecticut. If you murder someone, you may be sentenced to death in one state, but not in another state.

Most licenses are ruled by the state. Licenses for drivers, lawyers, accountants, nurses, teachers, and many others are state licenses. What is needed to get a license is often different from state to state.

What this means is that it is hard to get general information about most legal issues in the U.S. You can't get answers to questions such as "How old do you have to

1. Pieces of a puzzle

be to get a driver's license in the United States?" or "How are things divided up between people in a divorce?" In the U.S., a state is much more than just a way to break up the country into smaller parts. Unlike the Japanese prefecture, a state works almost like a separate country.

If you move to a different state, you have to apply again for a new driver's license. Even your will for after you die would not be effective if you move to live in another state. You need to make a new will according to the state you live in. It is no wonder there are so many lawyers in America.

A climate for everyone

Naturally, with such a large country, the climate will be different from coast to coast. Generally speaking, northern parts of the East Coast, including New York, have very cold winters. Southern parts of the West Coast, including California, have pleasant, comfortable weather all year around, and the South, including Florida, is hot and humid. The Southwest, which includes Arizona, is rather warm and very dry.

The differences in climate not only affect people's lifestyles, they also are attractive to a different type of people. Many retired people move to warm states such as Florida and Arizona. Some people who were born, grew up, and lived in New York move to California just for the nice weather, while other people, who enjoy the change of seasons, will move to the East Coast for its weather.

Still, whether it is hot or cold outside, you should feel comfortable inside. Buildings and public transportation are heated or air-conditioned. You may feel too cold, however, or too hot. It can be very cold in a movie theater in the summer, and you may sweat from the heat in a city apartment in the middle of winter.

Dreaming of warm beaches

New York is about as far north from the equator as Hokkaido or Aomori and has a similar climate. It is cold in the winter. The temperature may not go above 0 degrees Celsius for weeks at a time in January or February. There is snow and ice, and the wind and humidity may make it feel like it is much, much colder than the actual temperature.

In that kind of weather, all people think about is getting away from the unpleasant weather. Among people living in New York, vacations at the beach are far more popular than ski vacations. Even though beautiful snowy mountains are much closer than warm beaches, New Yorkers long for the warm weather. At Christmas, you will see displays in store windows for swimming suits. Spending time at a warm beach in the middle of winter is part of the good life for people living in New York.

South for the Golden Years

If you ask a middle-aged person from New York "Where do your parents live?" there is a good chance you will hear the reply "Florida."

In the U.S., people often change where they live as they move on to a new stage in life. A common pattern for an American goes like this: live with parents in the suburbs; leave parents' home to go to college;

after finishing school, move to city to start first job; after getting married, buy house or apartment in city; after having children, move to bigger house in suburbs; when children leave home, retire and move to different area.

Nice weather and low living costs are often what people think is important when they decide where they will live after they retire.

For the parents of baby boomers in the New York area, Florida is the most popular place to retire to. Elderly people in New York City are tired of having to clear the snow and of falling on icy sidewalks. Many of them, therefore, move south to Florida. Florida has a rather low tax rate, affordable housing, and most importantly, warm weather. As a result, many communities for retired people have developed in the state of Florida.

Such communities even have their own cultures, their own styles, and their own particular looks. You'll never see so many of the same type of car in any one place. There are Lincolns and Cadillacs all over. Both cars have a strong following of Americans over seventy years old.

All public places have many parking spaces for the

handicapped, not just the usual one or two spots seen in other areas. Early-bird dinners (discounts for dining at earlier-than-usual hours) are from 4 p.m. to 5:30 p.m., instead of the usual 5:30 p.m. to 7 p.m. This is because most older people keep earlier hours.

2. A land with an attitude
—getting a feel for the national spirit

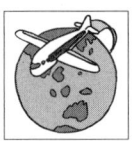

Freedom at a price

America has long been known as a country of freedom. Freedom is perhaps the word most commonly used when Americans describe the United States of America. In America, you are free to believe in anything, say almost anything you like, and hold almost any job. You are, generally speaking, free to do anything you like, as long as it does not break the law or get in the way of other people's rights.

It is wonderful to be free. However, freedom has its responsibility. More freedom for individuals also means that each individual must shoulder more responsibility. You therefore could say America is a country of freedom and a country of responsibility. It is easy to accept freedom. But it may not be so easy to accept the responsibility that comes with it.

2. A land with an attitude

American parents as a rule do not try to control the lives of their grown children. Even young children are treated more as individual people, not as a part of their parents or as the property of their parents.

American parents, however, do not usually provide financial support for their children once the children are grown. The children also don't usually live with their parents. Young people who can't afford their own places usually have roommates to help share living expenses.

Regardless of your age in the United States, there is generally more freedom. Age is not supposed to be important. You can apply for any job regardless of your age. On the other hand, life after you retire is largely your own responsibility. People know they cannot depend much on the government or on their children for help.

In America, you can't just sit and wait to see if things will happen. You have to act to get things done. You have to protect yourself. You have to speak out to be recognized. If you work hard, you have a good chance of getting what you want, but you still have to ask for it.

Success is respected in the U.S., no matter where you

are from. Everybody has the opportunity to be successful. *You have the opportunity to try anything because you are the one responsible for your life.*

No rosy picture

Do you think Americans have better social services than Japanese do? They don't. This is the country of every man for himself, the country of accountability, of holding yourself responsible. Here are some examples:

If you get hurt or fall ill suddenly and go to a hospital emergency room, the first thing you will be asked is which health insurance plan you have. There is no public health insurance except for the very poor or the elderly. You are expected to buy your own health insurance from a private company. The matter of cost is quite simple. Expensive plans cover more. Cheap plans cover less. Either way, you are responsible for all medical costs that are not covered by your insurance plan.

Having a baby and taking care of children are two other examples. If you have a baby, you are free to return to work the next day. You don't have to worry

2. A land with an attitude

about others talking about what kind of a mother you are. Still, there is no low-cost public system for taking care of children in the U.S. You will likely have to have a nanny, a person come to your home to take care of your child or leave your baby at a private childcare center. Either way, it will be quite costly. There is also no federal law giving you leave from work to have a baby. There are no free health checks or vaccines. *You must pay all the costs. It is your life and your child.*

English with an accent

Since America is a country made up of people from many countries, many citizens, naturally, came from different countries. You have different American accents from different parts of the country, and you can also hear people speaking English with many foreign accents. For example, you often hear English spoken with a Spanish accent or English spoken with an Indian accent in New York City. It may be hard to understand English when it is spoken with a heavy accent. You may not even realize that it is English when you first hear it or when people speak quickly. It also means, however, that most people in cities will not mind if you have an accent.

Though English is spoken almost everywhere in the world, there are still many types of English in the world. You do not have to speak like a television news announcer. Don't worry if your English pronunciation is not perfect. What is the perfect pronunciation anyway? It could be said the perfect American accent. Queen Elizabeth has heavy British accent and you have heavy Japanese accent. On the other hand, do not blame your imperfect pronunciation alone when your English does not work. The most important things are a desire and willingness to speak and communicate. If you have something you really want to say, you can always find a way. If you really want to understand someone, you will.

Although English is the only official language in the U.S., you will see Spanish in many public places. Because there are so many people from Spanish-speaking countries now living in the U.S., Spanish is the most frequently used foreign language in America. Many American businesses have Spanish service. You can

2. A land with an attitude

often choose between English and Spanish on ATMs (automatic teller machines) and ticketing machines.

But just because there is so much Spanish in the U.S. does not, by any means, mean that many Americans can speak both English and Spanish. Even though foreign language studies are required in high school, Americans do not generally speak any language other than English.

Americans expect you to speak English regardless of where you are from. People may approach you on the street to ask for help or directions. Just because you look Asian doesn't mean they assume you are Asian.

The kindness of strangers

America is an easy-going country. People do not expect you to always act a certain way. They usually respect the manners of another culture. From table manners to business manners, you don't have to worry about formal manners. Just use your common sense and you usually will be okay.

Americans are generally very friendly. People often smile at strangers. If you happen to make eye contact with a stranger you will most likely get a smile back. Strangers may talk to you in the street. People talk about the weather with strangers while waiting for a bus. Other shoppers may talk to you about new products at the supermarket. Such small talk makes things friendlier and brings on smiles. You can often get useful advice as well, such as whether something tastes good or where you can get a better price. Be open to small talk and enjoy it.

The friendliness you get from strangers, however, is not often the same attitude you will see with employees in stores and eating places. You may be surprised to get a dirty look from a worker at a fast-food restaurant. You will probably get far more social smiles than business smiles in the U.S.

Americans are not only friendly to strangers, they are also kind to them. When people see tourists looking at maps on the street corners, they will often ask if you need help. Mothers with baby strollers never have to carry them up or down the stairs at public places. People passing by always offer to help. When you are struggling with a big suitcase in a train station, somebody stronger

2. A land with an attitude

than you will almost always offer to help. In many cases, a kind stranger will help you more than the public systems themselves do.

It is expected that you, in turn, will help people in trouble in public places. If you don't, Americans may consider you cold and not very kind.

However, you do have to be careful around strangers. Think of your safety as well. Giving a stranger a ride in your car or helping someone out on the streets late at night is not usually a good idea. *Be street-smart.*

No smoking, please

America is a difficult country for smokers these days. If you visit a big city, such as New York or Los Angeles, you will have to make quite an effort if you want to enjoy a smoke. In New York, almost all public places are non-smoking. There are no smoking areas in restaurants. Even bars are non-smoking. The only place you can smoke may be on the street. You will see people smoking in front of office buildings in the cold of winter and the heat of summer.

It used to be good manners to ask "Do you mind if I smoke?" Now, nobody asks that anymore simply because smoking is not allowed in most places. Even if you were to ask, you would probably get "no" as an answer.

Actually, it is best not to ask, as you may sound desperate. Americans, in general, have a bad picture of smokers as being childish, undisciplined, unhealthy, and even uneducated.

For people who don't smoke and don't like smoke, America is heaven. Your clothes won't smell bad after you sit in a bar. In a restaurant, you won't be annoyed by the smoke from another table. *Indeed, it is easy to forget that there are people who smoke in the world.*

"Ladies first"—a subtle presence

American society respects equality and fair play. Women expect to be treated equally to men. The number of women who hold important positions in business, politics, and society in general has greatly increased over the last several years. One result of this that is not

2. A LAND WITH AN ATTITUDE

so nice, however, is that men are not as polite to women as they were before.

Is the idea of "ladies first" completely dead these days? It almost is, but not totally. Men no longer stand up when a woman comes into a room. But, most men will step aside and allow a woman to go in or out of a door before they do. Men still open doors for women. If you are on a first date with a woman, you will make a poor impression if you don't open the door for her.

"Ladies first" may no longer be so visible in the U.S., but it is still there. Here is a story as a perfect example:

A Japanese woman living in New York visited Japan with her son. They had lived in New York for more than twenty years. In Japan, her son received the attentions of many women. He was not particularly handsome, and he had not even had a chance to show off his language skills. He was an ordinary Asian man, except for one major difference—his manners. He would open doors and carry things for his mother. He would buy drinks for her, as well as for other women. This was seen as something quite unusual and attractive.

I heard another story from a young Japanese woman

who had worked in New York for five years. When on business trips in Japan, she is forever bumping into middle-aged men as she gets out of elevators. She is used to the men in New York waiting for her to get off the elevator before they do. The men in New York were doing what came naturally to them. The men in Japan were doing the same. This young lady remembered how, in Japan, she had always stayed in the elevator holding the door and waiting for everyone to get out ahead of her.

In the United States, if you are a man, you have nothing to lose by following the custom of "ladies first." *Making it a habit may give you the chance to be quite popular in Japan. If you are a woman, once you return to Japan, be careful going in and out of doors!*

3. Give me a break!
—the national holidays

The big ten

In the U.S., there are ten national holidays. Some holidays, such as Christmas and Independence Day are determined by the date. Others are set by the day of the week. These are mostly celebrated on Mondays.

The following are national holidays.

New Year's Day	January 1
Birthday of Martin Luther King Jr.	the third Monday in January
Washington's Birthday	the third Monday in February
Memorial Day	the last Monday in May
Independence Day	July 4
Labor Day	the first Monday in September
Columbus Day	the second Monday in October
Veterans Day	November 11

Thanksgiving Day	the fourth Thursday in November
Christmas Day	December 25

The most important holidays are **Thanksgiving** and **Christmas**. Most Americans get together with their families and have turkey for dinner. Most offices and stores are closed. The period between **Thanksgiving** and **New Year's Day** is usually called the holiday season. People take vacations to spend time with their families. People do a lot of shopping for gifts. Restaurants are packed full with holiday parties, both business and private. On the other hand, general business slows down, much as it does during the Japanese New Year's period. **New Year's Day** is the day people relax after the holiday rush. Most businesses start up again on January 2.

Around **Washington's Birthday**, also called **Presidents' Day**, many schools have winter break. So, the prices of air tickets and hotels tend to be high during this period. This also happens at the end of March around Easter when many schools have spring break.

3. Give me a break!

Memorial Day is a day to remember people who died in the service of the nation. It marks the beginning of the summer season. Barbecue parties are held all over the country. July 4, **Independence Day**, is a big time to get together too. Many towns and cities have firework displays on July 4. The summer season ends on **Labor Day**. Some people have barbecues to mark the end of summer. The new school year starts after Labor Day.

Columbus Day honors Christopher Columbus' landing in America. **Veterans Day** is a day to honor people who served in the U.S. military.

A matter of God

Even though Christmas is one of the biggest holidays in the U.S., it is still a religious holiday. There are people who do not celebrate Christmas because they are not Christians. Therefore, the greeting "Happy holidays" is heard as much as, if not more than, "Merry Christmas." There are many holidays, ethnic, religious, and non-religious, such as Hanukkah and New Year's Day, around Christmas time, "Happy holidays" is always a safe and fitting greeting.

Some examples of major ethnic and religious holidays around Christmas are:

Hanukkah——This is a Jewish holiday. The exact date will be different from year to year according to the Hebrew calendar but it usually falls in November or December. Hanukkah lasts for eight days. A candlestick with nine branches called a menorah is a symbol of Hanukkah. Instead of a Christmas tree and Santa Claus, Jewish children get presents each night for eight nights.

Kwanzaa——This is an African-American culture festival beginning on December 26 and ending on January 1. The festival was created in 1966 by Dr. Maulana Ron Karenga to help strengthen families, learn about one's roots, and about African-American history.

There are many families in the U.S. that have parents who came from different cultures. These families may

3. Give me a break!

celebrate more than one holiday during the yearend holiday season.

Red-letter days

There are many other days Americans celebrate. Although these are not legal holidays, they are special events for many people.

Valentine's Day, February 14——This is a day to celebrate love and romance. Couples exchange cards to express their love for each other, go out for special dinners, and exchange presents. Unlike the Japanese Valentine's Day, women do not give chocolate to men in general. Men are more likely to give presents, such as chocolates and flowers, to their lovers or partners. You can see men lining up at flower shops after work ends on Valentine's Day.

Mother's Day, second Sunday in May——This day is a day to show your respect and love for your mother and show that you are grateful for what she has done for you. Many mothers enjoy breakfast in bed on this day. Restaurants are packed on Mother's Day.

Father's Day, third Sunday in June——Fathers receive cards, phone calls, and presents from their children. Like in Japan, the day is less recognized than Mother's Day.

Halloween, October 31——This is an exciting day for children. Children get dressed up in costumes and go from door to door shouting "trick or treat!" and asking for candy. They usually come home with a lot of candy. The night before is called "Devil's Night" in many areas, and children and teenagers play pranks, such as ringing doorbells and running away, throwing rolls of toilet paper around people's lawns, or writing on car windows with soap. Adults also have costume parties on Halloween.

Kiss me, I'm Irish

Since America is a country made up of people from

3. Give me a break!

many cultural backgrounds and of many different religions, there are quite a few religious and ethnic holidays celebrated by various different groups of people. Many ethnic holidays are celebrated at schools as a way of learning about other cultures. However, religious holidays are not celebrated at schools. Here are some examples of religious and ethnic holidays.

Chinese New Year——This is the first day of the lunar calendar followed by Chinese, Korean, and Vietnamese. The date changes, but it usually falls between late January and early February.

St. Patrick's Day, March 17——This is a holiday celebrated by Irish Americans and many others as well, especially in cities with large Irish-American populations, such as New York and Chicago. Many cities have big St. Patrick's Day parades. The color green and the clover are symbols of the Irish. You will also see cookies and cupcakes with green icing.

Easter——This is a Christian holiday. The date will

change from year to year but always falls between March 22 and April 25. In addition to the Christian meaning of Easter, it also has other meanings. Eggs and bunny rabbits are symbols of Easter. Chocolates shaped like eggs and other Easter candies are sold everywhere. Children play games hunting for brightly colored hard-boiled eggs or plastic eggs filled with candy. For many people, Easter is a holiday to welcome spring.

Passover——This is a major Jewish holiday. The date will be different each year according to the Hebrew calendar but it always falls around Easter. Jewish families get together and have big special meals called Seder.

Fiddling with time

You have to change your clock twice a year in the U.S. Daylight Saving Time, also called Summer Time, starts on the first Sunday in April. The clock is turned ahead one hour. It means you lose one hour of sleep. Daylight Saving Time ends on the last Sunday in October. The clock is then turned back one hour. You get an extra

3. Give me a break!

hour of sleeping time.

The time is changed at midnight between Saturday and Sunday so there will be less trouble caused by the time change. The change in the fall usually does not cause people any trouble. Getting somewhere too early is not usually a problem. However, the beginning of Summer Time can cause trouble. Missing flights and being late for meetings is very common on the first Sunday of April.

4. All shapes, colors and sizes
—the American people

A quick look back

America is a country made of people of many races and many cultures. The earliest settlers in America were the people now called Native Americans. They were formerly called Indians, but this is no longer considered proper. For thousands of years, the only people living in America were these native peoples.

After Christopher Columbus' discovery of America in 1492, many Europeans began arriving in America. During the sixteenth century, the Spanish formed colonies in the southern part of what is now the United States. The French followed. From the 1600s, the English and the Dutch started to settle in the Northeast. In 1620, the Pilgrims from England came to America in the Mayflower to find and enjoy religious freedom. They formed a colony in Plymouth, Massachusetts.

4. All shapes, colors and sizes

The Dutch settled in New York. They made the famous purchase of Manhattan for only twenty-four dollars from the Native Americans. In 1619, the first African arrived in America. Later, many Africans came to America as slaves until after the Civil War, when it was no longer allowed to keep slaves.

The original colonies, the first thirteen states, declared their freedom from England on July 4, 1776. The final form of the Constitution of the United States was signed in 1787. It is the top law of the United States and helped to pull the government together. In the 1800s, the U.S. added new territory. Many people moved further west looking for land and looking to get rich. As the United States grew and people moved west, many Native Americans lost their land and their lives. Many were forced to move to faraway places where they were told they could live.

In the 1840s, there was very little food in Ireland. People were dying from hunger. This brought many Irish to the U.S. Lack of food in Germany also caused many Germans to come to the United States. In 1848, the

Mexican War resulted in a great many Mexicans moving to the southern part of the U.S. On the West Coast, the California Gold Rush brought a great number of people from China in the 1850s and '60s. The beginning of industrialization also brought huge numbers of people from Europe. Toward the end of the nineteenth century, large numbers of Italians, Poles, Russians, and Greeks raised the number of people from other countries who now lived in the United States.

In 1882, the Chinese Exclusion Act stopped Chinese workers from entering the United States. To replace the cheap labor the Chinese had provided, Japanese started moving to the U.S. In 1922, Japanese were told they could not become U.S. citizens. During World War I and the Great Depression from 1929 to 1941, the number of people moving to the U.S. dropped. Laws allowing people to move to the U.S. became stricter. There was also more unfairness based on race.

Following World War II, Asians were once again allowed to move to the United States. Chinese and Japanese were allowed again in 1952.

In 1965, immigration laws were changed. The new

4. All shapes, colors and sizes

policy allowed people to join their families and relatives again. People were also allowed to move to the U.S. based on their skills, not on which country they came from. Nowadays, the majority of people moving to the U.S. are from Asia and Latin America.

The original population of the U.S. had a large number of WASPs, or White Anglo Saxon Protestants, who originally came from Europe. WASPs today represent a much smaller percentage of the total U.S. population than they did before. There are also many African Americans, Asians, Latinos, Jews, and people from the Middle East.

Since people are often made up of a mix of race and culture, it is hard to separate the two. Race usually means the person's biological background. The U.S. Census Bureau lists six different races, "white," "black or African American," "American Indian and Alaska Native," "Asian," "Native Hawaiian and other Pacific Islander," and "some other race." These groups are based on biological histories rather than on a person's actual life. Europeans and people of the Middle East both fall in the same group, "white." Chinese, Japanese, Korean,

Filipinos, and Asian Indians also fall in the same category, "Asian." The most rapidly growing ethnic group, "Latino or Hispanic," could include people of any race. Therefore, "Latino or Hispanic" is not considered a racial group.

Racial issues in America used to be mostly about white and black. Although these issues still exist, the issues of today are even more complex. They include issues concerning peoples of many racial and cultural backgrounds. America used to be described as a "racial melting pot." Today, the expression "mixed salad," rather than "melting pot," is more often used. People with different backgrounds exist together without losing their own specialness. It is more important to respect the various different cultures and races than to blend together into one.

Talking about terms

Americans who came from Latin America used to be called Hispanic. The word Latino is more commonly used these days. However, neither term is clear. Usually, the word Hispanic is used to mean an American whose first language is Spanish. Latino means those Americans who came from Central or South America. Puerto Ricans, Cubans, and Mexicans are examples of Hispanic or Latino.

However, there are gray areas concerning these terms and many questions. Is a person of Spanish background Hispanic? What about Brazilian? Is he or she Latino? There have been discussions about these issues, but, as of yet, no official answers.

All in the family

America has so much world culture because most of its people came originally from countries all over the world. Usually, the second generation of these people became one with the society in general. However, their roots and the cultures of their ancestors, tend to live on as the family culture.

People who came directly from another country to the U.S. often tend to live together in communities of people of the same culture. For example, a large Russian community sprang up in Brooklyn when many Russians came to New York in the early '90s. The community and the type of people living in it change along with the different cultures.

The children born in the United States to these people usually do not stay in one particular community. Getting a better education and a good job is usually the aim of the children. *These goals are usually achieved through hard work.*

Pegged for a profession

Often, people from a certain country will tend to be attracted to one certain type of job or profession. For example, working as a gardener was once considered a common job for a Japanese on the West Coast some fifty years ago. Now many gardeners are Mexicans. Restaurants are often owned by Greeks. Usually, blue-collar jobs, labor jobs, are done by the people who are newer to the U.S. Some professions, however, are passed from parent to child. For example, many New York firefighters have Irish roots.

Splitting things up

Since each state in the United States stands alone in many ways politically, there are stronger differences between the different regions than in such countries as Japan. There are conservative states and liberal states.

The presidential race of 2004 showed this very clearly. It largely divided America into two parts, Red America and Blue America. Red America is the territory of the Republican Party and tends to be made up of the central states. Blue America is the territory of the Democratic Party, and is made up largely of the Northeast and the West Coast. Red America and Blue America could also be seen as rural America and urban America. Everyone knew before the election that the central states were conservative and the Northeast and the West Coast were liberal. The results of the election, however, made the differences even clearer.

A greater power

It is well known that Christianity is the main religion

of America. However, there are also people who are Muslims, Buddhists, Jews, and more. As the number of races and cultures grow in America, so do the number of religions. There are no public figures about religion because the government is not allowed to ask about a person's religion. You also cannot assume a person is a certain religion from the way he or she looks.

Religion can be a very sensitive issue. Public schools and workplaces are not allowed to favor one religion over another. So, it is important to separate cultural events and religious events in some cases.

Unlike the Japanese, Americans are clearer about their religious preference. If the person is not a Christian, Christmas may be just considered a normal day. There may be no Christmas tree, no Santa Claus. Instead, the person may take a day off for a holiday of his or her own religion.

In the blood?

Since Jewish is not considered a racial group, census figures do not show that there are many Jews in the

4. All shapes, colors and sizes

U.S. Although the Jewish population as a whole in the U.S. is rather small, Jews are a major cultural group in certain areas, such as New York. Jewish is supposed to be a religious group, but people tend to think of people as Jewish if they were born of Jewish parents. It does usually not matter if they practice Judaism or not.

Some Jews are very strict about following their religious rules. But some Jews do not even go to temples except for special family occasions, such as weddings and funerals. Some do not go at all. American Jews originally came from many different countries. Although blood ties are the most common way of saying who is Jewish or not, anybody can convert to the Jewish religion.

A means of support

Fairness and equality are important values in American society. Equal opportunity for both men and women is a respected rule. Most American women, especially those of the younger generations, have careers or want to have careers in the same way men do. The number of stay-at-home dads is increasing. However, there are still far fewer women than men in important positions in business, politics, and academics. Women also still spend long hours doing housework and taking care of children.

The paradox of the American policy on equality for the sexes comes largely from a lack of public support for having babies and caring for children. No discrimination toward women can mean no special support for women. It is not easy for women in the U.S. to have a career while raising a family.

American society is a society made for couples. Unlike in Japan, husbands and wives in the U.S. often socialize together. Married or not, being a couple makes things much easier on many social occasions. Single life is not as enjoyable as it is in Japan. This means that most single people are always looking for others to share their lives with.

Between the ages

America is one of the few developed countries not

suffering from a low birthrate. America is not an aging society. However, Americans are more separated by actual physical difference by generation than Japanese are. Most Americans do not live with their parents once they become adults. Also, people tend to move according to their life stages. Young people tend to live in urban areas. Parents and small children tend to live in areas that have a lot of families with children. Older people tend to move to special communities after they retire. Some of these communities do not allow families with children. On the other hand, areas that attract families with children who are going to school tend not to be attractive for older people and young adults. Since the cost for a good public school is high, property taxes in these areas are very high. As a result, people tend to move out after their children finish high school.

Recently, however, more senior citizens are living near their children. Some new developments are designed to be like old-style villages where different generations live together.

Boomers big business

People born in the period from after World War II to the early 1960s are usually the people who make up what is called the baby boomer generation. This age of people is the biggest group in the American population. People of this generation have created many of their own booms while growing up. They led the hippie movement, the women's rights movement, rock music, the economic boom of the eighties, and the real estate boom of the nineties. Because America is a nation of capitalism, more people means more business and more money. Marketing has always had its eye on baby boomers.

Senior power

The AARP, formerly known as the American Association of Retired Persons, is an organization representing senior citizens. With its almost fifty years of history, it is one of the biggest groups in the U.S. and has a great deal of influence. Its magazine, AARP, has the most number of copies of any magazine in the U.S.

4. All shapes, colors and sizes

This powerful organization has over fifty million members, and provides insurance services and discount plans for members. It has been a symbol of senior power in the U.S. However, it is struggling to get new members, aging baby boomers. Since anybody over fifty years old can be a member, the AARP is already looking at many baby boomers to get them to become members. It has still not succeeded to win over the generation of the "forever young."

We're all kin

Fifty years ago, American families could have been represented by the simple stereotypes seen on television shows. Dad goes to work and knows everything. Mom stays home with her apron on and keeps the home clean. The two or three children are always well dressed. However, this is no longer the case.

Variety is the word to describe the American family of today. Marriages between people of different races, different cultures, and different nations are increasing. Step families and single parents are also increasing because half of all marriages in the U.S. end in divorce. The ages of parents are also spread over a wider range than before. A family may have some adult children from an earlier marriage and a new baby from a second or third marriage. Families adopting children are common too. Children are adopted from overseas as well as from within the U.S.

Although the styles of families have changed a lot, having a family itself is still considered important for most Americans. America is a country made for families. This is part of the reason different family styles are created to adapt to a complex society.

Doing it differently

Recently, gay marriage has been a hot issue in the U.S. Although gay marriage is only allowed in a very small area of the entire country, there are many gay couples who live together as a family. Some of them also have children. Depending on the area, gay families can be socially accepted and open about their gayness.

Part 2

Part 2 gives you practical information
to help you get around
and enjoy your stay
in the USA!

読みはじめる前に

パート 2 で使われている用語です。わからない語は巻末のワードリストで確認しましょう。

- [ ] reception
- [ ] hospitality
- [ ] produce
- [ ] mobility
- [ ] eclectic
- [ ] donation
- [ ] bother
- [ ] ethnic
- [ ] vary
- [ ] occupancy
- [ ] sublet
- [ ] citizenship

知っておくと便利なアメリカの知識

liquor license 酒類を扱う場合に必要な証明書のことで、一般には市から認可を受ける。リカーライセンスがない店では客が自らアルコール飲料を持ち込むことが許されている。

American hospitality アメリカ人のフレンドリーな態度や、外部の人に対する温かいもてなしを表す。とくに南部の州(テキサス、ルイジアナ州など)で、このホスピタリティが息づいていると言われている。

return policy 購入した品物(とくに洋服など)を返品することはアメリカでは頻繁に行われる。そのため店側では、「〜日以内に返品のこと」などの条件をつけ(return policy)対応している。贈り物をする場合も、贈られた相手が簡単に返品できるように「渡す相手用のレシート(gift receipts)」まで用意されている。

tax deductible アメリカでは、病院、教育機関、美術館、博物館、バレエ団、オペラ劇場などの非営利団体への寄付は、免税扱いである。この制度が、企業や個人の寄付を募るために大きく役立っており、アメリカのアート界の活性化にもつながっている。

5. Reach out and touch someone
—communicating in the U.S.

I've got your number

Similar to Japan, the telephone is the most widely used communication tool in the U.S. In general, phone systems work almost the same as they do in Japan.

Phone numbers are made up of area codes of three numbers and local numbers of seven numbers. When you make local calls, you normally just dial the local number. In some big cities you have to dial the area code too. To make a long-distance call, you always have to dial 1 before the three-digit area code. To make a call to a toll-free number, you also need to dial 1 before 800 or 866.

If you don't know a phone number there are three ways to search for it. You can use a phone book. There are two kinds of phone books, the Yellow Pages and the White Pages.

In the Yellow Pages, phone numbers are listed by type of business. So, this book is useful to look for certain services or stores. For example, you can find lots of pizza shops under the word "pizza." However, if you are looking for a particular name, it is easier to look it up in the White Pages. Names are listed in the White Pages in alphabetical order.

You can also call directory assistance. To use this service, you need to know the name of the city you are calling.

Looking up phone numbers on the Internet is the easiest way to find a number. You do not have to talk to operators and you can take your time.

Finding one that works

As cell phones become more popular, the number of pay phones, also called public telephones, is becoming smaller and smaller. You can still, however, find pay phones on the street and especially at airports and train stations. Quite often, though, they are broken.

The cost of a phone call is always different depending

5. Reach out and touch someone

on the length and distance, but you can usually make a local call for a quarter (twenty-five cents). You can drop a quarter in the phone and dial the number you want to call. If you call a toll-free number, or make a collect call, the quarter will be returned at the end of the call.

Long-distance calls (calls to different area codes) can be a bit more difficult. Again, the cost will be different from place to place. Usually, with a pay phone, after you dial the number, a recorded message will tell you how much money you have to drop into the phone. This is not easy for foreigners. First, it is hard to understand the recorded message. Second, you need to have many coins, because long-distance calls from pay phones are quite expensive.

To avoid this problem, you can use a prepaid card to make phone calls from a pay phone. However, American prepaid cards are not like regular Japanese telephone cards. They are like prepaid cards for international calls from Japan.

Instead of putting in the card, you dial the number on the card and then follow what the recorded voice tells you to do. Usually, you input the prepaid number on your card and then dial the number you want to call. You may hear a recorded message. Do not get worried. Usually, the voice is just repeating what is written on the prepaid card.

Take your own

Like in Japan, many people have cell phones or mobile phones. However, the technology for the phones is not as good as it is in Japan and Europe. Not as many people in the U.S. use cell phones as they do in Japan and Europe. The phones generally do not receive signals as well, can do less, and are more limited in their use. The biggest problem is the weak signals. Even in New York City, there is poor reception in some areas. If you are inside a building you may not be able to get a signal. If you go to the suburbs, there are some areas where there is no reception at all. Although connections are good in most big cities, don't expect it to be the same as in Japan.

In the U.S., people generally only use cell phones for talking, not for exchanging data such as text messages or Internet information. One reason for this is

5. Reach out and touch someone

that Americans spend a lot of time driving, not using public transportation. They can't use the Internet or write text messages while driving. Another reason is that Americans use computers more than Japanese do. Americans tend to carry laptops or notebook computers with them. The weight and the size are not important because Americans are usually moving with their cars.

In any case, you will often not be able to exchange text messages with Americans through their cell phones. Instead, most people with cell phones use answering services, or voice-mail. *Since there are many places where there is no cell-phone reception, you will likely have many opportunities to leave voice messages.*

Surf's up!

Today, the Internet is one of the most important tools in the U.S. for communication and for getting information. Since English is the most common language on the Internet, countries where English is spoken have an advantage in using the Internet. People of all ages use the Net, from children to the very old. The Internet has become a necessary part of everyday life rather than only a hobby or luxury.

Children need to look up things on the Internet to do their homework. For adults, banking, paying bills, reserving movie tickets, making vacation plans, and shopping are all done by Internet. Since everything can be done without leaving one's home, it is particularly helpful for older people. However, the Internet is more widely used in the U.S. One of the reasons is Americans know how to use keyboards very well. Because there is a long history of typewriters, even older people don't mind typing instead of writing by hand.

For foreigners, the Internet also makes reservations and shopping easier. Reading what to do on a computer screen is usually easier than listening to telephone operators talking in foreign languages. You can take your time on the Internet. You can go back and read over something again and again.

Places where you can use the Internet, such as hotels, coffee shops and fast-food restaurants, are found everywhere. If you take your own laptop, you can check your e-mail and do searches in Japanese. However, computers at public places such as libraries, Internet cafes, and hotels usually do not support the Japanese language.

Silence is golden

E-mail is slowly taking the place of phone calls. This is happening not only in the business world but also in private life. College students talk with professors by e-mail. Children exchange information about homework by e-mail. The PTA sends out information to parents by e-mail instead of the phone chain that was used before. People also tend to prefer to send e-mail messages instead of leaving messages on answering machines. The average American adult spends more than one hour a day reading and writing e-mails. Young Americans may spend even more time. Unless you are quite old, it is hard to live without e-mail.

E-mail is also a great tool for foreigners. It is easier than talking on the phone in English. You can take your time and read and write something over and over if you need to. Most Americans have e-mail addresses. Just tell them you prefer e-mail to the phone. Most Americans have never experienced being a foreigner in a strange land. They may not realize that e-mail is easier to use than the telephone for people whose first language is not English.

Let your fingers do the talking

As mentioned earlier, most Americans use cell phones only for talking, not for sending text messages. However, many American children and young adults talk through text-messaging on their cell phones. They also tend to use instant messages on their computers a lot.

Sending text messages by cell phone is a rather new service in the U.S. Teenagers have started using it more and more. Cell-phone text-messaging is slowly becoming more popular in the U.S.

Sending it 'snail'

These days, letters and other things sent by the post office are often called "snail mail." This is because of the slowness in getting to the person you are sending it to as

5. Reach out and touch someone

compared to e-mail and other hi-tech communications. Still, people exchange holiday greeting cards, pay bills, and send business and personal papers through the postal system. It is still one of the least costly and widely used means of communicating.

Post offices are usually open from 8 a.m. to 5 p.m. Monday through Friday. Some offices are open on Saturday until 1 p.m. Regular mail is usually delivered once a day from Monday through Saturday except for holidays. Mail delivery service is different from area to area. In rural areas and many suburban areas, mailmen not only deliver mail to you, they will also pick up mail you wish to send. They will pick it up from your mailbox, provided your mail has the correct number of stamps on it. In some rural areas, you have to pick up your own mail at the local post office.

City post offices often have long lines of people waiting. Sometimes, slow workers and cool attitudes can be annoying. On the other hand, in small towns, the post office can be an important part of the community. Workers and customers often know each other and exchange small talk while picking up or sending mail.

By sea or by air

For mail sent within the United States, there are many different classes. The most commonly used class is first-class. This is for regular mail, for sending letters and postcards. Second class is used for mailing certain publications. Third class is limited by weight (up to one pound) and is for letters and other printed material. Fourth class is for packages weighing between one pound and seventy pounds.

Priority mail is faster than regular mail and can be used for either letters or packages. Express mail is the fastest and the most expensive, but it is the same in both speed and price as private services.

Americans often insure letters or packages sent by mail even if the letter or package is not especially valuable. The rate you pay depends on the amount you want to insure your mail for.

If you need a receipt of delivery to show that the mail has gotten to the person you sent it to, ask for registered mail. If you need a receipt of sending to show that you have sent the mail, ask for certified mail.

5. Reach out and touch someone

When mailing things overseas, there is both air mail and surface mail. For faster service, you can also use priority mail and express mail when sending things overseas.

Lost without a ZIP

All addresses in the United States have ZIP (zone improvement plan) codes. A ZIP code is made up of between five and nine numbers. The first five numbers are necessary for sending mail. The ZIP code is also very useful for searching for something on the Internet. The code is given to only a small area in the U.S., so knowing it can give you better results than just searching for something by the name of the town or city.

You will often be asked for your ZIP code, such as when doing business with the bank or when shopping, so it is a good idea to know it.

Money in the bank

Unlike Japanese post offices, the U.S. postal service

does not operate savings accounts for people or provide insurance policies.

Money orders can be bought at the post office. Though they are not commonly used, they are good for people who don't have checking accounts or credit cards but who need to make a payment by mail or by using something other than cash.

American citizens also apply for passports at local post offices.

6. Getting where you want to go
—transportation in the U.S.

Fly me

Traveling by plane is the most common way to travel long distances in the U.S. Because America is a huge country, one must usually travel by air for both business and pleasure. Also, train systems in the U.S. are not as well-developed as the Japanese train system. In the U.S., people take a plane as easily as they take the bullet train in Japan. Americans often use airplanes for business trips or family vacations. There are even some people who go to work by airplane.

Competition between airlines is increasing. There are more and more airlines with cheap flights. So, there is a great choice of airlines, routes and fares.

Generally speaking, the earlier you buy your ticket, the better the price. If you buy a ticket at the last minute, you may have to pay more than twice the price of a discount ticket.

There are many ways to purchase airplane tickets. The easiest way is to buy them from a travel agent. You can get special discount rates too. Another way is to buy them directly from the airlines. Many airlines have special discount plans or mileage plans for people buying tickets online. You can also purchase tickets from many online agencies.

Prices for plane tickets in the U.S. are pretty reasonable compared to Japan because flying is a common and casual form of transportation. There is, however, a bad side. You cannot expect to receive much service unless you fly business class. If you are very choosy about your food you had better bring your own.

Airports are always crowded. Flight delays and cancellations are common. It is wise to check often when your plane is expected to leave or arrive, even when the weather is perfect. If your flight is canceled, do not just sit there and wait. You should act quickly in order to get another flight, reserve a hotel room, or whatever you need to do to save your trip. Since problems are common, nobody will come and help you. You have to look

6. Getting where you want to go

for help yourself. After it is announced that a flight has been canceled, you will see many people rushing to the ticket counter. *Americans know what they have to do and do it quickly.*

Being safe

Since the U.S. has been hit by terrorist attacks, airport security has become much tighter. Anything that could be used to hurt others, especially something sharp, is not allowed on board. The search at the gate is strict too. You will likely be asked to take off your shoes. Laptop computers are checked one by one.

To avoid having your bags lost and to reduce waiting time at the baggage claim, many people prefer to carry their bags on board instead of checking them. However, the rules for carry-on bags are quite strict now. Be careful about the size and about what is in your carry-on bag.

Because of the security checks, there are often long lines of people waiting to enter the gates area. You need extra time. At major airports, there are many shops and restaurants inside the security-check point. If you get inside too early, it is easy to kill time waiting for your flight to leave.

On the rails

Traveling long distances by train is not common in the U.S. Even though Amtrak has a rail system across the country, people do not often use trains for traveling long distances. The main reason for this is that it simply takes too much time. Because the train system is not used much, it is not well-developed. Because it is not well-developed and not convenient, people don't use it.

Commuter trains, on the other hand, are widely used in big-city areas on the East Coast. Going to work by train is a good way to avoid getting caught in heavy traffic. American commuter trains are much less crowded than commuter trains in Japan. They are also more comfortable. People riding the train can read or work on their laptops. However, there are fewer trains. For example, Metro North, one of the New York area trains, only runs twice each hour during the busiest

6. Getting where you want to go

hours and once an hour at other times of day.

Each railroad company has a different ticketing system. For Metro North, many stations have no workers. Passengers buy tickets from a machine and the tickets are checked on the train by conductors.

Going underground

Heavy traffic is a problem all over the world. But no matter where you are in the world, people use public transportation in the big cities. Many big cities in the U.S. have subway systems and New York City has the biggest subway system in the country. However, you cannot expect the trains to be on time. New York subways come whenever they come. Although the trains run quite frequently, you cannot depend on them. In Tokyo, a twenty-minute delay of a subway train would make the evening news. In New York, a delay of twenty or thirty minutes is common.

A ride on the subway in New York costs two dollars, regardless of the distance you travel. Nowadays, prepaid cards are most commonly used. You can buy prepaid cards from a ticket machine or from the ticket booth at a subway station. Cash or credit cards are accepted. I recommend using a credit card because cash often causes trouble with the machines. Either the bills won't go in or the machine gives you the wrong change.

Unless you ride subways very late at night, there is no need to feel insecure on the train. However, it is still wise to sit in a car where there are other people and avoid being alone. You will usually be with others, as many people ride the subways. In most cases, subways are the fastest way to get around the city.

Watch where you're going

Many tourists love buses. You can see outside and feel safe. It is hard to miss your stop because you can see where you are going. Buses also stop more frequently than subways do. They can get you closer to where you want to go, and you can avoid walking long distances.

Buses are the easiest to use of the different means of public transportation. You can use them with a wheelchair too. It is also easy for older people and people with

6. Getting where you want to go

small children to get on and off buses.

There are disadvantages to using a bus though. You cannot depend on them time-wise as much as you can with subways. Buses are usually the slowest form of transportation. During rush hour, it may even be faster to walk.

The way you pay your fare or buy your ticket is different from city to city. In most cases, you use tokens or prepaid cards. If you pay in cash, you need to have the exact amount. Bills are usually not accepted because you cannot receive change. If you plan to travel around a city by bus, it is a good idea to buy tokens or prepaid cards in advance.

Door to door

Taking a taxi, which is also called a cab, is an easy way to get around the city. It gets you where you want to go with ease even if you don't know the city. There is no need to walk in the cold on a winter night or in the heat on a summer afternoon. The down side of a taxi is its cost. It is the most expensive means of transportation in the city. And, although it is often the fastest way to get where you're going, sometimes heavy traffic can slow things down.

Taxis are usually not fancy. They often have a beat-up look, worn or torn seats, and sometimes broken air conditioners. The doors do not open by themselves. Do not stand and wait for the door to open when you get a taxi. And do not forget to close the door when you get out.

Limousine or hired cars are a little fancier than taxis. You call a limousine company and a car provides door-to-door transportation. Limousines or hired cars are generally more expensive than taxis. However, you may get better rates than a taxi when traveling to popular places such as the airport.

Just for fun

Unlike in Asian cities, bicycles are not often used as a means of transportation in the U.S. In the big cities in the United States, there are no safe parking spots for bicycles. In rural or suburban areas, the distances traveled to work or shopping are usually much greater than those you would want to travel by bicycle. In America, bicycles are generally for exercise and for fun. About the only people who use bicycles as a means of transportation are messengers, such as are often seen in New York City.

The pedicab, which looks like a tricycle with a carriage, is the newest kind of transportation in New York City. Pedicabs are much like a cross between a taxi and a horse carriage. They are both a means of transportation and a form of entertainment. They usually charge by the minute, at about one dollar a minute.

No car, no life

For Americans, not having a car means not being able to get places. New York City may be the only city in the U.S. adults can live easily without a car. In other areas, a car for each adult is common. Young and old, men and women, Americans drive every day. In fact, being able to drive more or less determines how well a person can get along. For teenagers, getting a driver's license means mobility and is a big step toward being able to live on one's own. When elderly people give up driving, many of them start thinking about "assisted living," or getting people to help them.

Americans love cars. Most Americans spend hours in their cars every day. They use cars to go to work, school, shopping, friends' houses, doctors, restaurants, simply everywhere. In suburban areas, most mothers who don't work outside of the home drive about one thousand miles a month. People who drive to work or school may drive even more miles every month. Cars are often like a second living room for families. Children do homework and eat dinner in cars on the way to their lessons or sports practices. Cars are often like moving offices for adults.

The reason Americans spend so much time in their cars is because it is more or less necessary. Except for in a few cities, such as New York, there is often nothing within walking distance. And in most areas of the U.S., public transportation is limited.

Because it's often impossible to get around without cars, rental cars are often necessary. Renting a car is often a part of business trips or family vacations. There are many car rental places near airports. Roads are generally very good and it is not difficult to drive in the United States. You will likely get used to it very quickly.

Licensed to drive

As I mentioned before, a driver's license is issued by each individual state. Therefore, what is needed in order to get a driver's license is different from state to state. In most states, you cannot use a foreign driver's license to get a local one. You may use an international driver's license. However, the international one is often not recognized in the U.S. It is a good idea to have both your international license and your regular driver's license from your own country with you.

A driver's license is used not only for driving, but also as I.D. in many situations, such as getting into a club, buying alcohol or cigarettes, using checks, returning purchases, and much more. In many cases, your regular driver's license is required as well as the international one.

Beware of buses

Although traffic rules, such as speed limits, are different from state to state, the basic rules are the same. For foreign drivers, one of the important rules other than driving on the right side of the road, is the rule about school buses. When you see a school bus stopping to pick up or drop off children, you are not allowed to pass the bus, whether it is coming toward you or going away from you. If the bus is coming toward you, you must stop and wait for the bus to pass you before you can move again. When you are following a bus you must wait for it each time it stops. *This can be quite a bother, but don't break this rule unless you want to get in trouble.*

So many words!

In the U.S., driving directions are usually given in words rather than as a map. Many Americans prefer written directions to maps. Even on Mapquest, a popular free driving-direction Web site, you get only simply drawn maps, but detailed written directions. It is a bit of

6. Getting where you want to go

problem for foreigners because maps are much easier to follow than written sentences. If you ask Americans driving directions for getting somewhere, they will either tell or write the directions, instead of drawing a map.

"Take Exit 7 (Route 7 North) exit and drive thirteen miles north to New Milford. Follow 202 east to the right and cross steel bridge. After three traffic lights, road splits to Route 202 East and Route 67 South. Make a left on to Route 202 East. Continue on Route 202 East. Brookside Avenue will be on the right-hand side of the road just after the IGA supermarket parking lot."

You will likely need to try hard to understand and then keep such directions in your head, as it is almost impossible to drive while reading them. It is a good idea to buy a detailed map of the area you plan to drive in. A good map will help you get around a strange town and make it much easier to follow driving directions. When you have a map you can correct your route even if you make a wrong turn. In the U.S., every street has a name or a number, and street signs are on almost every corner.

7. A place to lay one's head
—where to stay

Rooms by the night

Making a reservation is necessary in most hotels. Even when there are empty rooms, most hotels do not like to have people come in asking for a room without a reservation.

Staying at hotels is expensive, especially in big cities. If you plan to stay for just a few days, a package tour that includes your hotel may be the best deal for you. If you plan to make a reservation by yourself, check the hotel to see if it offers any discount plan. Many hotels do.

Generally speaking, staying in hotels on weekends is cheaper than on weekdays. If you can, it is wiser to include weekend nights in your stay to keep the cost down. You can also check airlines and credit card companies for any hotel discounts they may offer. If you plan to stay longer than a week in the same area, ask if

7. A place to lay one's head

there are any special rates, such as weekly rates, for a longer stay.

There are many ways to make hotel reservations. You can call the hotel or check the hotel's Web site on the Internet. Or, you can work with a travel agent or use an Internet hotel reservation service. It is always a good idea to look around for the best rate.

Be careful, however, about the conditions for stays. In many cases, the rates that are given in ads are based on double occupancy, in other words, you have to be traveling with someone else. The price given is for one person but you have to pay for two. You may be charged double if you travel alone or you will at least likely be charged more than the price given. You should also make any special requests, such as for a no-smoking room or for an extra bed, when you make your reservation.

In most cases, you need a credit card in order to make reservations. Take the same card to the hotel with you when you check in. The check-in process is usually simple and easy. It's a good idea to have single dollar bills for tipping various employees, such as those who carry your bags or call a taxi for you. If you do not have small bills, it is a good idea to get change at the front desk when you check in.

Eating at a hotel is expensive and usually not the best eating in town. Unless you have a special meal plan included in your hotel rate, it is a better idea to eat elsewhere. Even in the city, you can have a nice breakfast for under five dollars.

A place of your own

If you plan to stay in one area for a long time, you may consider renting an apartment or a house. The shortest length of a contract is usually one year for a house or apartment. Some landlords ask for two years. In some cases, such as when renting a summer house, you may be able to get a contract for a few months. The rents for staying only a short time tend to be higher than those for year.

To find a place to rent, look for ads in local newspapers or go to a real estate agency. Answering an ad in a newspaper yourself may help you save money as you won't have to pay the agent anything. You will likely be rent directly from the owner. Working with an agency, on the other hand, can give you more choices. An agency can also help you find what you want more easily in an area you don't know.

If you are planning to stay for a few weeks to a few months, subletting is another choice. Subletting means getting a lease from the person who usually lives in the apartment while he is away on an extended vacation or living somewhere else for a while. This way, you can often get cheaper rates than you would for a place of your own for only a short time. To look for a place to sublet, check local papers, bulletin boards in stores or Web bulletin boards.

Sharing the fun

Apartments in U.S. cities are getting more and more expensive. Rents in major cities, such as New York, San Francisco, and Los Angeles, are getting higher and higher. A month's rent for a studio apartment (a small apartment usually made up of one main living space, a small kitchen, and a bathroom) can easily cost fifteen hundred dollars in New York. An apartment with one bedroom can cost more than two thousand dollars a month.

More and more young people are choosing to share with someone. If you have very little money to spend on where you live, your only choice will be to share.

You can find roommates in the ad section of local newspapers, on Web sites, and on bulletin boards at stores. If you are a student, your school's student office may help you to find someone. A good roommate can make your life more fun and add much to your experience while staying in the United States. A bad roommate can make your life awful. It is important to be sure that you can get along with the person and be safe with him or her. You must also remember that you will have to give up some of your space and privacy.

Many people now share with someone of the opposite sex, especially if they have more than one roommate. It is never a good idea to share with someone who is not the same sex as you if that person is a total stranger to you. Safety should always be your first concern.

7. A place to lay one's head

My home is your home

Staying at someone's home as a guest is a great way to get to know the American way of life. Houses in the U.S. tend to be big, except in a few big cities where real estate prices are very high. Many American homes will have a room set aside for guests to stay in. There, you will be able to enjoy nearly as much privacy as you would in a hotel room. However, most homes do not have people to help with the cleaning or other housework. Basic manners require that you keep your room and bathroom neat and clean yourself.

"Make yourself at home" is one of the basics of American-style hospitality. Americans will treat guests like family members. The warm, friendly atmosphere is very nice. However, don't forget that being comfortable is not the same as being lazy. Try to help cut down on the work for the person you are staying with. Help around the house with whatever would please your host.

And, remember, don't stay past your welcome. There is an old saying: After three days, guests and fish smell bad. Don't be a smelly fish!

8. Chowing down
—where the food is

'A party for two'

Although America is not known for fancy eating, there are quite a few great restaurants, especially in big cities. You can have excellent dining experiences while enjoying a variety of different types of cooking. Years ago, eating at an expensive and fancy restaurant meant eating at a French restaurant. Not any more. Most of the most popular restaurants take an eclectic approach to eating, in a style sometimes known as contemporary American. These restaurants serve many unusual, yet tasty, dishes based on a variety of ethnic cooking styles, including French. Italian, an American favorite, is much fancier these days. Japanese and other Asian dishes are also featured at many trendy restaurants.

Reservations are necessary at fine restaurants, Some restaurants require your credit card numbers when you

8. Chowing down

make a reservation. This is so they can charge you for cancellations made at the last minute or if you don't show up.

Some popular restaurants are booked for dinners at the most popular times for more than a month in advance. If the restaurant is open for lunch, reservations for lunch may be a little easier to make. You may also find it easier to get a reservation at popular restaurants for dinner at very early (5 p.m.) or late (10 p.m.) hours. If you still have trouble getting a reservation and you are set on getting one, try the restaurant bar. Some fine restaurants serve food at the bar. "First come, first served" is the rule at the bar in any restaurant. So, if you arrive early enough, you have a good chance of getting a seat at the bar.

Fancy pants

"Jackets required" used to be common at fancy restaurants. Nowadays, fewer and fewer restaurants have such dress codes. However, not being strict about what customers must wear does not mean you can wear anything you please to a fancy restaurant. Looking neat and clean or wearing fashionable clothes is a part of the experience of eating at fine restaurants in the U.S.

Never go to a fancy restaurant wearing your everyday clothes such as jeans and running shoes. Those are fine for a pizza shop or an inexpensive ethnic restaurant. But trendy restaurants, even if the dining style is "casual," require you to be dressed better. If you don't meet the dress code you probably will not be kicked out, but you may feel out of place. And, worse, you may make the person you are eating with feel bad. If you are not confident about fashionable casual wear, just wear a suit and tie or a nice dress. It is always safer to be dressed too well than not well enough.

That down-home feeling

There are two kinds of casual restaurants in the U.S. One kind of restaurant are those owned by national restaurant chains. These restaurants are largely aimed at families. The other kind is the individual, privately owned restaurant. The good thing about eating at one

8. Chowing down

of the major chain restaurants, such as Red Lobster, Applebee's, and TGI Friday's, is that you get the same dishes and tastes anywhere in the country.

The not-so-good thing about the national restaurant chains is that one's choices can be limited and rather boring. On the other hand, the good thing about privately owned restaurants is that you may have delicious food at a reasonable price. You may, however, have a dining experience you would rather not have.

In big cities, you can find a lot of privately owned, individual restaurants that serve great food. In a suburban or rural area, you need to check around in order to be sure to find a good restaurant. You may, however, get lucky and chance upon a great restaurant in a small town. The best hamburger restaurants tend to be along some old road somewhere, not in the middle of a big city.

Usually, you do not need a reservation to eat at a casual restaurant, unless it is a trendy restaurant in or near a city. Many of these restaurants post their menus in their windows or on their front doors. You can check them out before you decide to go in.

Keeping it simple

In every town, there is a diner or a coffee shop. These eating places serve simple American food such as sandwiches, soup, salads, and hamburgers. Food is usually quite plain and menus are almost always the same wherever you go. Inside, things are usually quite warm and pleasant.

They are also very popular as breakfast spots, especially on weekend mornings. You will be seated and right away served coffee, tea, or a juice of your choice. Favorite breakfasts for Americans are either a plate of pancakes or two eggs in any style, served with fried potatoes and toast.

Diners and coffee shops are a good choice for people who do not like fast-food restaurants but still want to eat at a casual, simple restaurant.

Taste from the Old Country

You can find cooking from all over the world in the U.S. The most popular ethnic food is Italian. In fact, it has

8. Chowing down

been popular for so long that no one really thinks of it as ethnic. Pizza and pasta are the two most popular dishes in the U.S. in both restaurants and at home.

Chinese food is also very popular. Chinese restaurants are everywhere. Mexican cuisine is also very common. The food at these ethnic restaurants, however, may not be much like the food that is served in the original countries. Still, it is usually reasonably tasty and rather cheap.

Big cities, such as New York City, have almost every kind of ethnic food, and many of the restaurants serve food very much like the food in the original countries. Some, however, will create new and interesting dishes. In any case, there are many ways to enjoy ethnic foods, from the food served at cheap food stands to the creations of fine restaurants.

The areas where you are likely to find ethnic restaurants have been changing as the popularity of such foods increases. The best Chinese restaurants are not necessarily to be found in Chinatown. The best way to find a good ethnic restaurant is to ask people who came from that particular country.

One big, happy family

Family-style dining, sharing plates of food set out on the table, has become popular in recent years, especially at Italian restaurants. Usually, one dish is big enough to share with two or three people. If you want to taste many dishes, get together with four or five people and share. Family-style restaurants are casual and, naturally, welcome families. Some of them do not take reservations except for big groups.

Bringing the kiddies

American society is pretty children-friendly. Children and babies are welcome at most restaurants, except very fancy ones. Many casual restaurants have a special children's menu with food that appeals to children, such as pieces of deep-fried chicken and plain pasta. If you don't see a children's menu, ask the waiter if there is anything especially for kids. They may offer something even though they don't put it on the menu. Or you can ask what may be suited for children. Most restaurants will also be able to help you with simple requests for children. Also, there are usually high-chairs for babies or raised chairs for small children if you ask for them.

BYOB

Restaurants in the United States need a liquor license to serve alcoholic drinks. Sometimes, a new restaurant will open without a liquor license because of the long time needed to get one. In this case, you can bring your own drink to the restaurant. Since restaurants make a big profit on the alcohol they sell, if you bring your own, you will be saving a lot of money.

Closest to the 'conbini'

Delicatessens, or delis, as they are commonly called, sell food that can be eaten right away. The most common things sold at delis are sandwiches with cold cuts, cuts of roast beef, pastrami, ham, and smoked turkey breast. Customers order the kind of bread they want and the kind of filling, such as cold cuts or cheese, and condiments such as mayonnaise, mustard, or ketchup. Delis are a great place to have your favorite sandwiches made for you.

The sandwiches are usually huge and very filling and make a great lunch, especially if you're quite hungry.

Little Seoul

Korean delis are small stores owned by Koreans. They can be found on almost every street corner in big cities like New York, San Francisco, and Los Angeles. They are open twenty-four hours a day and sell everything you need for everyday life. The Korean deli is similar to the convenience store in Japan. Unlike convenience stores, however, most Korean delis sell many kinds of fresh produce, such as fruits and vegetables. They are also known for their salad bars, which include Asian food. They tend to be more expensive than supermarkets.

Hamburger heaven

America is the home of the fast-food restaurant. Some

8. Chowing down

American fast-food chains, such as McDonald's and Kentucky Fried Chicken are found all over the world. Even though they are representative of the American food culture, not many tourists go to them because such eating places are already so well-known.

Although the fast-food restaurant is not especially nice in the city, it can have its appeal in rural areas. In a small town in the middle of nowhere, it may be quite nice to be able to eat food you know. It may not be a great eating experience, but you do know what to expect.

Not all fast-food restaurants belong to national chains. There are many smaller chains that are unknown outside the United States or outside a certain region. It can be fun to try one of these local fast-food chains. Local people often love these places. They are not gourmet or health-food by any means, but you can find something enjoyable and usually cheap.

On the pavement

It can be fun, especially when the weather is nice, to buy

food from people selling food on the street. Buying food from street stands is cheap, quick, and easy. And some of the food really tastes good.

Hot dogs are the food most commonly sold on the street in the U.S. You can find hot-dog stands on the streets in many towns. Hot dogs are one of America's favorite fast foods and a common food "to go." Usually they are cheap, less than two dollars each, and easy to eat while you are walking.

Pretzels are another favorite food sold on the street. These are soft pretzels, not the hard kind eaten in handfuls as snacks. Some people like to eat them with mustard.

In the winter, the smell of honey-roasted peanuts fills the streets, and in the summer, ice cream trucks ring their bells to call children to them. Some of the trucks only sell packaged ice cream and ice cream bars. Others also have machines for making soft ice cream cones.

In some city areas, you will also find ethnic food stands—Middle-Eastern, Chinese, Mexican, and others. They sell good food at reasonable prices. If you walk around a busy city area at lunchtime, you'll see street vendors. If people are waiting in line for the food, it is probably worth trying.

9. Big bucks, little bucks
—where to spend your money

Variety's the name

Department stores in the U.S. are similar to Japanese department stores. Cosmetics and fashion accessories such as ladies' bags and scarves are usually to be found on the ground level of the store. Ladies' fashion floors and men's fashion floors are usually on the floors directly above.

Stores also have a children's section and a home section, and some of the bigger department stores have a furniture floor. However, although there may be a coffee shop or simple restaurant, there is no restaurant floor in American department stores as there is in Japanese department stores. Also, toys and stationery are not likely to be found in U.S. department stores.

What is nice about shopping at department stores is that you can shop for many different kinds of things

9. Big bucks, little bucks

and not be approached all the time by salespeople. What is not so nice about shopping in department stores is that you often can't find a sales clerk when you do need one. To avoid this, it's a good idea to go to the stores during those times when they are the least busy. It's a good idea to avoid the weekends. Monday through Friday in the mornings is a good time to find help easily. Unfortunately, no matter what day of the week it is, some stores that are not so popular may not have many employees. You won't see many shoppers, but you also won't find many salespeople.

Something special

Specialty stores tend to be more expensive than big stores like department stores. But the salespeople tend to be much nicer in smaller stores. You will surely get more attention and service. If you are just looking around, the friendly salespeople can be a bother. If you are looking for a particular thing, or if you need help, they can be quite helpful. As a rule, the salespeople know quite a bit about the things sold in their shops.

The employees in the smaller stores often work for a commission, meaning they receive a percentage of the sales they make. Naturally, they are serious about getting you to buy. *America is a country of equal treatment. If you have money and spend it, you'll be treated well—no matter who you are.*

All under one roof

You can see shopping malls all over the United States. Most of them look just like the next one. The mall is really an American style of business itself. The mall is perfectly suited to the American way of life, which revolves around the car. In the suburbs, shopping almost always means a trip to the mall.

Most shopping malls have at least one or two major department stores, if not more, and many shops of national brands. Except in urban areas, the malls tend to be long buildings surrounded by huge parking areas.

The malls are built around the department stores, either with them in the middle or at the ends, or both. Small shops line the central halls. Food courts, which

9. Big bucks, little bucks

offer a variety of fast-food to eat there or take home, are usually to be found in the center of the mall.

Some of the larger malls have areas for children to play, often with rides and game machines.

Malls also often have movie theaters and fine restaurants. The shopping mall is often the town's entertainment center. You can easily spend all day in one mall.

You can find the same national brand shops all over the United States in shopping malls. If you watch the flow of customers into a shop, you can get a good idea of shopping trends. Malls are great places for seeing where young people like to shop. They are also a favorite place for suburban teenagers to hang out.

Shopping malls, however, may not be very interesting for some shoppers, especially the shopper wanting to find unique things to buy. Malls are usually just full of very ordinary things. A few malls have luxury brands or names from Europe, but you will not find an unusual boutique like you would find in downtown New York City. Still, malls are the best place to experience the American way of shopping.

Taking it back

The biggest difference between Japanese and American shopping customs is in returning things purchased at the store. In America, returning purchases is almost a part of shopping.

In Japan, people almost never return things they bought unless they find something wrong with their purchases. In the United States, people often return things simply because they change their minds and no longer like what they bought. It is acceptable to return things for no real reason at all, as long as you follow the store's policy.

Each store has a different return policy, but returning things if they are not used, or if they are in the original wrapping, is acceptable at most stores. If you have lost the receipt, or if the thing you are returning was a gift, you can still return it at most stores. In that case, however, you are likely to only get store credit, not money back. When you come home from shopping and are not sure if you will keep the product you bought, keep the wrapper and the tags on. Also, be careful when buying

9. Big bucks, little bucks

things on sale. Often the sales are final, meaning no returns are allowed.

The days after Christmas are known as the busiest week for returns because people return Christmas presents. Most Americans are quick to return gifts if they do not like them. Although many stores accept returns without receipts, the new practice of gift receipts is becoming more common. You get a gift receipt with your gift which allows you to return the gift if you like. *Being able to return the gift is, in a way, part of the gift.*

Finding the bargains

Outlet malls are probably the most popular shopping place for tourists. They are huge and fun to shop in. You can spend the whole day shopping. You can buy famous brands at reasonable prices.

One good thing about the outlet mall is that you can depend on it. It is always there. Almost everything is offered at reasonable or reduced prices.

On the other hand, outlet malls can easily cause you to spend too much. And, you are not likely to find the latest fashions at an outlet mall. You may discover that you have bought a lot of unnecessary things.

You can often get very good prices at regular stores and department stores when they are having sales. There are certain times of the year when there are major sales, for example, right after Christmas. Naturally, the problem with this is timing. You have to be at the right place at the right time. Knowing about sales means you have to stay on your toes and watch for notices of sales. *It's a lot of work, but you may just get lucky!*

Also, many of the national chains have regular sales racks, where prices are reduced even though the store is not having a special sale. The sales racks are usually in the back of the shops. Check them before you look around at the regular-priced sections.

Nature calling

Generally speaking, there are fewer public restrooms in the U.S. than in Japan. Most department stores have restrooms only on certain floors. The best way to find out where they are is to ask the workers.

9. Big bucks, little bucks

Usually, the ladies' rooms are in the corner of the ladies' fashion floor, the men's rooms are on the men's fashion floor. In a big mall, there should be more than one place for restrooms. There are always some near the food courts.

In suburban areas, you can find public restrooms in almost any store, including supermarkets. In the cities, supermarkets do not usually have public restrooms.

Supermarket insights

If you are visiting the U.S. as a tourist, you may not need to go to a supermarket at all. However, the supermarket is a very interesting place, and a great place to get to learn about American culture and way of living. You can see how Americans cook, eat, and clean. You can shop at a supermarket without saying a word. You can examine package labels for as long as you want, and, most importantly, you can enjoy your shopping experience without spending a lot of money.

Most supermarkets accept credit cards as well as cash. Be careful about getting on the line for cash only. These lines are often found at busy supermarkets. There may also be express lines for people only buying a few things.

At the cash register, you have to take everything out of your cart or basket and put it on the counter. Don't just put the whole basket on the counter.

If you pay with a credit card, you may have to slide it through a machine.

Most supermarkets have people who will put your things into bags for you. You can ask for what type of bag you would like, paper or plastic. *The plastic bags are usually much weaker than Japanese plastic bags, so be careful!*

Finding fun souvenirs

Buying good souvenirs, especially things you can't find in Japan, can be very hard. The supermarket, however, is one of the best places to find interesting gifts at low cost. Supermarkets carry products used in everyday life, and this, in turn, can lead to interesting talks about food and American life. For example:

Junk food for children: The candy section is where

9. Big bucks, little bucks

you will find many different shapes and colors. For holidays, makers will come out with special holiday candies; black and orange candy shaped like monsters for Halloween; green and red for Christmas; pink and red candy, and candy shaped like hearts for Valentine's Day, chocolate eggs and wrappings in pastel colors for Easter.

Cereals: Americans love cereal. You will be surprised to see the huge rows of boxes of cereal. Most of these cereals are full of sugar and aimed at children. Among them, however, are some fairly healthy ones, too.

Instant foods: There are many sauce mixes, instant noodles, and snacks that you can't find in Japan. These are also generally light and easy to carry with you back to Japan as souvenirs.

Crazy days

From right after Thanksgiving Day up until Christmas Day, everyone shops in America. Americans are crazy about holiday shopping. The amount of money people spend during the holidays is taken as an indicator of the economic conditions in the U.S. Manufacturers and retailers think up ways to get as much business as possible during the holiday season. Thus, there are many special sales all over the country at this time.

The day after Thanksgiving Day is known as the busiest shopping day of the year. On that day, all stores open very early in the morning, at 6 a.m. or 7 a.m., or even earlier. There are special sales for early shoppers. Stores are packed all day long, and some people spend the whole day doing their holiday shopping.

After Christmas Day, comes the biggest sales week of the year. The stores are busy and packed with sales hunters and people returning gifts. It is not until the second week in January that stores finally get back to normal business.

Biggest of the big

Since the 1980s, mega stores and discount stores have increased their share of the American retail market.

9. BIG BUCKS, LITTLE BUCKS

This is not just a trend within the U.S. The mega stores and discount stores can be found in Japan as well. But, like the country itself, the American mega stores and discount stores are supersize.

A mega store is a huge store that deals mostly with things in one category. Unlike department stores, mega stores may have things in just one area, but they have almost everything in that area. Staples and Office Max, for example, are for office supplies. Barnes & Noble is for books. Home Depot is for hardware.

If you go to Home Depot to buy a nail, you may feel like you are lost in a sea of hardware. Not only does the store have hundreds of different kinds of nails, it also has wood, doors, windows, bathtubs, tools, paint—everything needed to build a house.

These stores often offer better prices than the small shops. They also make it easy to get all your shopping done if you have a big project. They are not always good for small shopping though. If you only want one nail it may be quicker and easier to go to a local hardware shop than Home Depot. If all you want is a notebook, it may be easier to go to a small drugstore than to Staples.

Discount stores, such as Wal-Mart, Kmart, and Target, are also popular places to shop. They offer discount prices for many kinds of products and are similar to supermarkets and department stores in the non-food products they sell.

There is another style of discount store called the wholesale club. Wholesale clubs, such as Costco, are also called warehouse stores. They charge membership fees and offer wholesale prices. The prices are good for everything, from produce to furniture. Unfortunately, you have to buy in bulk. You have to buy twenty-four rolls of paper towels or five avocados instead of just one or two. It is a good place to buy things that you can stock.

10. Getting in on the action
   —sports and the arts

Take me out to the ball game

The three big sports in the United States are baseball, basketball, and football (American football, not soccer, which is called football elsewhere). Of the three sports, the one closest to the hearts of Japanese is baseball, especially now with Ichiro, Hideki Matsui, and many other Japanese players active in the Major League.

As of 2005, some thirty teams belonged to the Major League, which is divided into two leagues—the American League and the National League. Each team plays 162 games each season, at the end of which the teams with the best record play to win the pennant for their league. Then, the pennant winners play in the World Series, a best-of-seven series which decides the national champion.

Not only Americans play in the Major League. There

are also many Puerto Rican players, Cuban players, and, now, with Japan leading participation from Asia, many Japanese players. In the U.S., if you're good, you can play, regardless of your citizenship.

Most night-time Major League games start between six and seven o'clock in the evening. Day games begin around noon. Like in Japan, the season begins in April. Weather-wise, states such as Florida and California have little problem, but April on the East Coast is likely to still have many cold days. If you're unlucky you may find yourself shivering in the stands, even with a down jacket on. American baseball parks, unlike the domes in Japan, are almost all open-air. If you're going to games early in the season, go prepared to beat the cold.

Since many Americans go to the games with their cars, ball parks are sure to have big parking lots. During the long days of summer, you'll no doubt see people gathering in the lots before the games and having barbecues, eating and drinking and having a great time, as if they were having a regular picnic. You'd even think, and you may be right, that a lot of people have come more for the tailgating than for the ball game. Tailgating, by

10. Getting in on the action

the way, is named after the back of the car. The kinds of cars that open in the rear and give you a place to sit are ideal for these "car picnics."

If you have a chance to visit the States, try to get to a ball game. With a hot dog in one hand, a coke or beer in the other, root loudly for the team of your choice. *You're sure to have fun. It's the real thing—and a truly American experience!*

A high-class mix

You can see many kinds of performing arts in the U.S. and enjoy some of the world's top performances. From classical theater arts such as opera and ballet to experimental performances, you can see not only American artists but great artists from all over the world.

Although tourists don't often go to modern dance performances, there are many great modern dance companies in the U.S. In fact, America is where modern dance was born. Modern dance performances and small theaters are more casual than classic performing arts performances and Broadway musicals.

Getting in the door

There are several ways to buy theater tickets. You can buy tickets by phone or you can buy them over the Internet. Either way, you have to pay a ticketing charge for each ticket you buy, and you need to have some information ready to give when you make the phone call or use the Internet.

You need to give your billing address. This is usually the same as your mailing address. You also need to give your credit card number and the expiration date of your credit card.

It is sometimes difficult to spell out foreign addresses quickly so it is a good idea to write down your billing address in English letters before you place your order on the phone. This will make it easier to tell the operator your address.

Tickets will be sent to you so they arrive before the show date. If the show date is too close, you can pick up your ticket at the theater. Be sure to bring the same credit card with you to the theater that you used to buy the ticket. They will just look at it and give it back to you. It is used as a form of identification and is an easy way to buy tickets. Not many words are needed.

You can also buy tickets directly at the theater. This way, you do not have to pay a ticketing charge. However, the ticket windows at theaters are only open at certain times of the day and getting there at the right time may be hard.

Although tickets for theater performances tend to be expensive, there are often ways to get discount tickets or ways to cut costs, especially in the big cities.

In New York City, the discount ticket booth for Broadway shows is famous. There is always a long line of people waiting to get tickets at half the regular price. However, there are other ways to get cheap tickets. Look for discount coupons for Broadway shows. These coupons can sometimes be found at school offices, local libraries, and in various stores. In the middle of winter, which is the off-season as far as sightseeing goes, you may find advertisements for special discount plans for all Broadway shows. There are different ways of getting the discount. Two common examples are "Buy one, get one free" and "Half price for kids."

Most theater performances start at 8 p.m. Only certain performances, for example, those that especially appeal to children, such as the ballet "The Nutcracker," start earlier in the day. On weekends, matinees are from around 2 p.m. Restaurants in the theater areas often have special menus for before performances. These are usually less expensive than the regular dinner menu. Food is served quickly so people can be sure to be in time for the show.

Tickets for opera, ballet and classical music concerts are particularly expensive. However, you can save money by buying season tickets, a series of tickets for all the performances held that year. Season tickets are sold before regular tickets, through advance sale. This allows you to often get better seats as well.

Catching a flick

Watching movies is a favorite American thing to do. The latest movie always makes for good conversation. Movie theaters are much more casual than performing arts theaters. There are many types of movie theaters all over the country—from a small theater in a small town to a huge theater with a huge screen.

Prices of tickets will vary from theater to theater, but tickets are generally much less expensive than movie tickets in Japan.

You can see only one show for a ticket. You can't stay in the theater once the movie ends and watch it again for free. Tickets are sold for each show time. Although movie tickets do not have assigned seats, movie theaters sell tickets for only the number of seats. There are no tickets sold for standing room only. So, once the tickets for a particular show time are sold out, you have to wait until the next show time. People line up to buy tickets before the starting time. Buying tickets in advance or on the Internet is becoming more common. Buying through the Net is nicer because you do not have to go to the movie theater early and wait in line.

Finger-lickin' good!

Movies and popcorn go together for Americans. At the beginning of the movie, you can hear the sound of people eating popcorn all over. In fact, the sales of popcorn and soda pop make up a big part of revenues for movie theaters. Sometimes, the money people spend on food and drink at the movies is more than the cost of the movie ticket alone. But people still line up for a big bucket of popcorn and a large cup of soda. The connection between eating and drinking and watching movies may be something that comes from childhood memories. And, you're likely to start doing it too. At first, you may not like the idea of a huge bucket of popcorn. But if you try it once, you may find that a year later you won't be able to watch a movie without eating.

Where the art is

There are many great museums in the U.S. Some of them are really huge and you may get lost in them. Many are free. Many of them offer guided tours. The first time you visit a certain museum, it is a good idea to join a guided tour. After the tour, or the next time you visit, you can walk around on your own. Very big museums, such as the Metropolitan Museum of Art in New York

10. Getting in on the action

City, have many different kinds of guided tours. You can choose the one that interests you. Some museums even offer tours in foreign languages, including Japanese.

It is better to avoid a featured exhibition unless you are particularly interested in it. Special featured exhibitions tend to be crowded. You have to stand in lines and try to get a look at the paintings between other people's heads. Go to regular exhibition rooms on weekday mornings. Major museums have enough masterpieces to make great regular exhibitions. You may find that some weekday morning, say, in the middle of January, you will find yourself sitting all alone in the center of a room of the Met. And there will be nothing and no one between you and Van Gogh's "Irises." *What a luxury!*

Gift shops, too, are great places to go in the museums. Most museums today put a lot of thought into their gift shops and many offer original products that reflect the art in the museum. The gift shops are excellent places to buy souvenirs.

Supporting the system

America has a system to support art. There are many public grants to support young talented artists. Private individuals and companies give money to museums and theaters. Donations for non-profit organizations are tax-deductible. With many organizations you can become a patron of the organization by giving a certain amount of money. You can then get special benefits such as invitations to special events or priority seating at performances. There are enough individuals and companies who prefer giving donations to paying tax. Thus, this system can work. To try to get donations, organizations make great efforts to appeal to people. This circle of effort, appeal, happy viewers, and donations helps keep American art and performing arts strong.

11. Money makes the world go round

The green stuff

American society has been called a cashless society for a long time. Americans depend on credit cards and personal check for their everyday lives. Still, you do need cash for many occasions, especially in the cities.

You need cash for taxis, cash for a hot dog from the street stand, and cash for food from a deli. You will want to have some cash when you just want to kick around town. Once you leave the big city areas, finding a place to exchange foreign money is not easy. Banks that change money are not common, not as common as in Japan.

Bills (most common are $100, $50, $20, $10, $5, $1)

Since cash tends to usually be used for the payment of

small amounts, it is not common to use big bills, such as the fifty-dollar bill or the hundred-dollar bill. In fact, there are some stores that will only take twenty-dollar bills or smaller. You can't use a hundred-dollar bill the same way you would a ten-thousand-yen bill in Japan, even though the amount is nearly the same. So, it is a good idea to get smaller bills when you exchange yen for dollars. For payments bigger than twenty dollars, you can probably use your credit card almost everywhere. Also, ATMs are open twenty-four hours a day. You do not need to carry a lot of cash. For safety reasons, it is also not a good idea to carry a lot of cash.

The most commonly used coins are: quarter, twenty-five cents; dime, ten cents; nickel, five cents; penny, one cent.

Coins are also called "change," and each individual coin is usually called by its name, such as a quarter or a dime, rather than by its value, such as twenty-five cents or ten cents. This can take a while to get used to. The quarter may be thought odd by many Japanese, perhaps because they are used to the metric system based on units of ten. Why break a dollar into fourths? Nowadays, because the rates and prices of everything have gone up, the quarter is used more than ever. You will need them for pay phones, washing machines, and parking meters, to name a few.

The money system is often used to teach American children simple math, so people are used to figuring payments using a quarter dollar as a unit. Often, when an amount is broken down, it is rounded to the nearest quarter. To make a payment of seventy-seven cents, for example, non-Americans may break up the amount into fifty, twenty, and seven in their heads. But Americans tend to break it up into three quarters and two pennies as this method makes use of the coins that can be used.

Do you take checks?

Personal checks are commonly used in the U.S. Almost all adults have them. They are used much like bank transfers are used in Japan when making payments, such as electricity, gas, water, taxes, and mail-order shopping. Checks are also used for personal payments to friends or as gifts to relatives on birthdays. Checks are also used for getting cash at stores.

You must have a checking account at a bank to have personal checks. These accounts may require a fee, but that can often be dropped if you keep a certain amount of money in the bank.

Don't leave home without it

A credit card is a must in the U.S. You will need credit cards for buying, for renting, and for making reservations. You can use your Japanese credit cards in the U.S. in the same way you would use them in Japan. At many stores, you will often have to slide your credit card through a card-reading machine and select a payment type. For payment type, choose "credit," not "debit," unless you have a debit card from an American bank.

To tip or not to tip

Tips cause a lot of trouble. How much to leave as a tip is always a question, even for Americans. Is it too much or too little? The amount never seems to be just right. The general rule is a tip is supposed to be fifteen to twenty percent of the total bill. The smallest amount for a tip other than at a restaurant is usually a single dollar bill.

Although you are supposed to give a tip for most sorts of services, you are not expected to pay the owner of a business for services. For example, you would give your hair stylist at a beauty shop a tip, but not if he or she were the owner. Of course, you may already be charged more for having your hair done by the owner than by one of the employees.

You can include the tip in your payment when paying with a credit card at a restaurant or beauty salon. You do not need cash in these instances. At hotels, however, you should have a supply of single dollar bills to tip here and there for services, such as for the bellboy.

When you've got a beef

The amount of a tip you give should show, generally, how happy you were with your service. However, leaving no tip or a very small tip is not the best way to deal with bad service. If you are very unhappy with the service, it makes more sense to call the manager and explain what the problem was. It may help to right the situation, and you even may get something as an apology for your unpleasant experience.

About the Author

In 1987, Motoko Kuroda, a native of Tokyo, decided to take leave from her work as an advertising copywriter in order to further her English skills. She arrived in a small college town in Massachusetts knowing no one and knowing next to nothing about life in the United States.

When the pickup service from the school she was to attend failed to show up at the airport in Boston, Kuroda panicked. She didn't know how to make a long-distance call from a pay phone. She didn't even know what a quarter was. Fortunately, a stranger helped her get a cab to the school.

Kuroda has been living in the United States ever since. Her initial plan of one year of study evolved into graduate school and work as a freelance writer and translator. She then started a family.

After a few months in Massachusetts, Kuroda moved to New York City, and later a suburban area some 100 km away. Her encounters with Americans and American living tend to have been acquired chiefly in the New York area, and though she has tried to generalize information where possible, she reminds readers that life is different all over the States.

Kuroda's years of experiences in the U.S. prompted her to share what she feels is some of the most important information for people visiting the country. This book, *Enjoy Your Visit*, is the first of a two-part series. *Enjoy Your Visit* is written with the short-term stay in mind, for tourists, students, and businesspeople. The book includes general information about the U.S. and specific practical information for visitors, Japanese in particular. For more information on longer stays and everyday life, Kuroda encourages you to read her second book, *Enjoy Your Stay*.

Word List

- 本文で使われている全ての語を掲載しています（LEVEL 1、2）。ただし、LEVEL 3以上は、中学校レベルの語を含みません。
- 語形が規則変化する語の見出しは原形で示しています。不規則変化語は本文中で使われている形になっています。
- 一般的な意味を紹介していますので、一部の語で本文で実際に使われている品詞や意味と合っていないことがあります。
- 品詞は以下のように示しています。

名 名詞	代 代名詞	形 形容詞	副 副詞	動 動詞	助 助動詞
前 前置詞	接 接続詞	間 間投詞	冠 冠詞	略 略語	俗 俗語
熟 熟語	頭 接頭語	尾 接尾語	記 記号	関 関係代名詞	

A

- **AARP** 略 全米退職者協会（=American Association of Retired Persons）
- **academic** 形 学園の、学校の 名 大学生（教官）、学問的環境
- **accent** 名 アクセント、口調、なまり
- **accept** 動 ①〜を受け入れる ②〜に同意する、〜を認める
- **acceptable** 形 受諾（容認）できる、満足できる
- **accessory** 名 付属品、装飾品、アクセサリー
- **according** 副 ①《- to》〜によれば［よると］②〜に従って、基づいて
- **account** 名 ①説明（書）②勘定（銀行の）口座 動 〜を…とみなす
- **accountability** 名 責任（範囲）、説明義務
- **accountant** 名 税理士、会計士
- **achieve** 動 成し遂げる、達成する、成功を収める
- **acquire** 動 ①（努力して）獲得する ②（学力、技術などを）習得する
- **act** 名 ①行為、動作 ②法令 動 ①行動する ②機能する ③〜を演じる
- **active** 形 ①活動的な、活躍している ②積極的な ③活動［作動］中の 名 （組織の）現役
- **actual** 形 実際の、現実の
- **adapt** 動 〜に適合させる、順応させる
- **add** 動 〜を（…に）加える、足す
- **addition** 名 付加、追加 in addition 加えて、さらに
- **address** 名 ①住所 ②演説 動 ①〜にあて名を書く ②〜に演説をする
- **adopt** 動 ①採択する、選ぶ ②承認する ③〜を養子にする
- **adult** 名 大人、成人 形 大人の、成人した
- **advance** 名 進歩、前進 動 進む［進める］、進歩する［させる］ 形 先行の in advance あらかじめ、前もって
- **advantage** 名 ①有利な点［立場］動 〜に有利に働く、〜を促進する
- **advertisement** 名 広告、宣伝
- **advice** 名 忠告、助言、意見
- **affect** 動 ①〜に影響する ②（病気などが）〜を冒す 名 感情、欲望
- **afford** 動 《can -》〜することができる、〜する（経済的・時間的な）余裕がある

124

Word List

- **affordable** 形 手ごろな(良心的な)価格の
- **African** 形 アフリカ[人]の 名 アフリカ人
- **African American** アフリカ系アメリカ人(の)
- **agency** 名 代理店, 仲介
- **agent** 名 ①代理人[店] ②代表者
- **aging** 形 年老いた, 老朽化した 名 老化, 年老いること **aging society** 高齢化社会
- **aim** 動 ①(武器・カメラなど)を向ける ②〜をねらう, 〜を目指す 名 ねらい, 目標
- **air-conditioned** 形 エアコン(空調)のきいた
- **airline** 名 航空会社
- **Alaska** 名 アラスカ《地名》 **Alaska Native** アラスカ先住民(の)
- **alcohol** 名 ①アルコール性飲料, 酒 ②アルコール
- **alcoholic** 形 アルコールの, アルコール性の 名 アルコール依存症
- **allow** 動 ①〜を許す ②〜に…を与える
- **along with** 〜と一緒に, 〜と同調して
- **alphabetical** 形 アルファベット順の, ABC順の
- **although** 接 〜だけれども, 〜にもかかわらず, たとえ〜でも
- **American football** アメリカン・フットボール
- **American Indian** アメリカインディアン[語], アメリカ先住民
- **American League** アメリカン・リーグ, ア・リーグ《野球》
- **American-style** 形 アメリカ式の
- **amount** 名 ①量, 額 ②《the-》(〜の)合計 動 (総計)〜になる
- **Amtrak** 名 アムトラック《全米鉄道旅客輸送公社の名称》

- **ancestor** 名 先祖, 祖先
- **announce** 動 〜を(人に)知らせる, 公表する
- **announcer** 名 アナウンサー
- **annoy** 動 いらいらさせる
- **anybody** 代 ①《疑問文, 条件節で》誰か ②《否定文で》誰も(〜ない) ③《肯定文で》誰でも
- **anymore** 副 《通例否定文, 疑問文で》今はもう, これ以上
- **anywhere** 副 どこかへ[に], どこにも[へも], どこにでも
- **apology** 名 謝罪, 釈明
- **appeal** 動 ①〜を求める, 〜を訴える ②(人の)気に入る 名 ①要求, 訴え ②魅力, 人気
- **Applebee's** 名 アップルビー《全米外食店チェーン》
- **apply** 動 ①申し込む, 志願する ②あてはまる ③〜に適用する
- **approach** 動 ①〜に接近する ②〜に話を持ちかける 名 接近, (〜へ)近づく道, アプローチ
- **apron** 名 エプロン
- **Arizona** 名 アリゾナ《地名》
- **artist** 名 芸術家
- **as far as** 〜に関する限り, 〜の範囲までは
- **as long as** 〜する限りは
- **as of** 〜現在で, 〜以後は
- **as of yet** まだ今のところ
- **Asia** 名 アジア
- **Asian** 名 アジア人 形 アジア[人]の
- **aside** 副 わきへ(に), 離れて
- **assign** 動 任命する, 割り当てる 名 譲り受け人
- **assist** 動 手伝う, 列席する, 援助する **assisted living** 介護生活
- **assistance** 名 援助, 支援
- **assume** 動 ①〜と仮定する, 〜を当然のことと思う ②〜を引き受ける

Get to Know the USA: Enjoy Your Visit

- **ATM** 略現金自動預け払い機（=automatic teller machine）
- **atmosphere** 名①大気 ②雰囲気, 周囲の状況
- **attack** 動①~を襲う, 攻める ②~を非難する ③(病気が)~を冒す 名①攻撃, 非難 ②発作, 発病
- **attend** 動①~に出席する ②~の世話をする, ~に仕える ③(学校などに)行く, 通う
- **attention** 名①注意, 集中, 注目 ②配慮 間《号令として》気をつけ
- **attitude** 名姿勢, 態度, 心構え
- **attract** 動引きつける, 魅力がある
- **attractive** 形魅力的な, あいきょうのある
- **automatic** 形自動の, オートマチックの
- **average** 名平均, 並み 形平均の, 普通の 動平均して~になる
- **avocado** 名アボカド
- **avoid** 動~を避ける, ~をしないようにする
- **awful** 形①ひどい, 不愉快な ②恐ろしい 副ひどく, とても

B

- **baby boomer** ベビーブーマー（世代）《1945年から60年代生まれ》
- **background** 名背景, 前歴, 生い立ち
- **baggage** 名手荷物 baggage claim 手荷物受取所
- **ballet** 名バレエ, バレエ団
- **ball park** 野球場, スタジアム
- **bar** 名①バー, 酒場 ②棒, かんぬき ③障害(物) 動①~をかんぬきで閉める
- **barbecue** 名バーベキュー
- **bargain** 名①バーゲン(品), 安売り ②駆け引き
- **Barnes & Noble** バーンズ＆ノーブル《全米書店チェーン》
- **base** 名基礎, 土台, 本部 動基礎を~に置く
- **baseball** 名野球, ベースボール
- **basic** 形基礎の, 基本の 名《-s》基礎, 基本, 必需品
- **basketball** 名バスケットボール
- **bathroom** 名トイレ, 浴室
- **bathtub** 名浴槽
- **beat** 動①~を打つ ②~を打ち負かす 名打つこと, 鼓動, 拍
- **beat-up** 形おんぼろの, くたびれた
- **beauty** 名①美, 美しい人[物] ②《the -》美点 beauty shop (salon) 美容院
- **bedroom** 名寝室
- **beef** 名①牛肉 ②筋肉, 強さ ③《米俗》請求書 ④不平, 苦情
- **beer** 名ビール
- **bell** 名ベル, 鈴, 鐘 動①(ベル・鐘が)鳴る ②~にベル[鈴]をつける
- **bellboy** 名(ホテルなどの)ボーイ
- **belong** 動《- to》~に属する, ~のものである
- **benefit** 名①利益, 恩恵 ②《失業保険, 年金などの》手当, 給付(金) 動利益を得る, ~のためになる
- **best-of-seven** 名7回戦制で4勝したチームが勝ち
- **beware** 動用心する, 注意する
- **big-city** 形大都会, 大都市
- **bill** 名①請求書, 勘定書 ②法案 ③紙幣 ④ビラ big bill 高額紙幣 動①~に請求書を送る ②~を勘定書に記入する billing address 請求書送付先の住所
- **biological** 形①生物学(上)の, 生物学的な ②血のつながった
- **birthrate** 名出生率

Word List

- **bit** 名①《a – of》少しの～、1つの～ ②小片 **a bit** 少し、ちょっと 動 bite（～をかむ）の過去、過去分詞
- **blend** 動混合する、溶け合う、調和する 名混合物
- **blood** 名①血、血液 ②血統、家柄 ③気質
- **blue-collar** 名形 ブルーカラー（の）、肉体労働者（の）
- **board** 名①板、掲示板 ②委員会、重役会 動①～に乗り込む **on board**（船・飛行機などに）乗っている
- **book** 動記帳する、予約する
- **boom** 名①ブーンという音 ②ブーム、急成長
- **boomer** 名ベビーブーム世代（の人）、一時的な人気者
- **booth** 名ブース、売店、切符売り場
- **boring** 形退屈な、うんざりさせる
- **bother** 動～を悩ます、困惑させる 名面倒、いざこざ、悩みの種
- **boutique** 名ブティック、専門店
- **branch** 名①枝 ②支流、支部
- **brand** 名ブランド、商標、品種
- **Brazilian** 名ブラジル人 形ブラジル人の、ブラジルの
- **brightly** 副明るく、輝いて、快活に
- **Broadway** 名①ブロードウェイ《通りの名》、ブロードウェイ劇場街 形ブロードウェイ（風）の
- **Brooklyn** 名ブルックリン《地名》
- **Brookside Avenue** ブルックサイド・アベニュー《通りの名》
- **bucket** 名バケツ
- **buck** 名（略式）ドル、1ドル
- **Buddhist** 名仏教徒 形仏教（徒）の、仏陀の
- **bulk** 名①大量、大部分 ②積み荷
- **bullet train** 新幹線
- **bulletin board** 掲示板
- **bump** 名①衝突（の音）②こぶ、隆起 動①《– into》ドスン［バン］と当たる ②～に（と）ぶつかる［ぶつける］
- **bunny rabbit** ウサギ、ウサちゃん
- **BYOB** 略飲み物持参、飲み物持ち込みのパーティ（=Bring your own bottle）

C

- **cab** 名タクシー
- **Cadillac** 名キャデラック《車名》
- **cafe** 名コーヒー［喫茶］店、カフェ
- **calendar** 名カレンダー、暦
- **California** 名カリフォルニア《地名》
- **cancel** 名取り消し、使用中止 動取り消す、中止する
- **cancellation** 名キャンセル、取り消し
- **candlestick** 名ろうそく立て
- **capitalism** 名資本主義
- **card-reading machine** カード読み取り機
- **career** 名①（生涯の、専門的な）職業 ②経歴
- **carriage** 名①馬車 ②乗り物、車
- **carry** 動（品物を）店に置く
- **carry-on bag** 機内持ち込みバッグ
- **cart** 名荷馬車、荷車、（スーパーなどで使う）カート 動～を運ぶ
- **cash** 名現金（払い）動①～に現金で支払う、～を換金する **cash register**（店舗内の）レジ
- **cashless** 形現金のいらない、現金のない
- **casual** 形①偶然の ②略式の、カジュアルな ③おざなりの
- **category** 名カテゴリー、種類、部類
- **celebrate** 動①祝う、祝福する ②

127

Get to Know the USA: Enjoy Your Visit

祝典を開く
- **cell phone** 携帯電話
- **Celsius** 名形 摂氏(の)
- **census** 名 一斉調査, 国勢調査
- **cent** 名①セント《米通貨。1ドルの100分の1》②《単位としての》100
- **central** 形 中央の, 主要な 名《C- America》中央アメリカ
- **cereal** 名①穀物 ②シリアル, コーンフレーク
- **certain** 形①確実な, 必ず～する ②(人が)確信した ③ある ④いくらかの 代～の中のいくつか
- **certified mail** 配達証明付き郵便
- **champion** 名 優勝者
- **charge** 動①(代金)を請求する ②(…を)～に負わせる 名①請求金額, 料金 ②責任 ③非難, 告発
- **check** 動①～を照合する, ～を検査する ②～を阻止[妨害]する ③(所持品)を預ける ④～を調べる 名①照合, 検査 ②小切手 ③(突然の)停止, 阻止(するもの) ④伝票, 勘定書 checking account 小切手用口座
- **check-in** 名 宿泊(搭乗)の手続き
- **cheese** 名 チーズ
- **Chicago** 名 シカゴ《地名》
- **chiefly** 副 主として, まず第一に
- **childcare** 名 保育, 児童保護 形 育児の, 保育の childcare center 保育所
- **childhood** 名 幼年[子供]時代
- **childish** 形 子供っぽい, 幼稚な
- **children-friendly** 形 子どもに優しい
- **china** 名①陶磁器, 瀬戸物 ②《C-》中国
- **Chinatown** 名 中国人街《中国本土以外で中国人が集まって暮らす場所》
- **Chinese** 形 中国[人]の 名 中国人[語]
- **Chinese Exclusion Act** 中国人排斥法《1882年に成立した中国人移民を制限することを決めた法令》
- **Chinese New Year** (中国の)新年
- **chocolate** 名 チョコレート
- **choice** 名 選択(の範囲[自由]), 選り好み, 選ばれた人[物] 形 精選した
- **choosy** 形 好みのうるさい, 選り好みする
- **chow down** 食事を取る
- **Christian** 名 キリスト教信者 形 キリスト教(徒)の
- **Christianity** 名 キリスト教, キリスト教信仰(精神)
- **Christmas (Day)** クリスマス
- **Christopher Columbus** クリストファー・コロンブス《人名》
- **cigarette** 名 (紙巻)たばこ
- **circle** 名①円, 円周 ②循環, 軌道 ③仲間, サークル 動 旋回する, 囲む
- **citizen** 名①市民, 国民 ②都会人, 住民, 民間人
- **citizenship** 名 市民権
- **Civil War** 南北戦争《米1861-65》
- **classic** 形 古典的の, 伝統的な 名 古典
- **classical** 形 古典の, クラシックの
- **clear** 形①はっきりした, 明白な ②澄んだ ③(よく)晴れた 動①～をはっきりさせる ②～を片づける ③晴れる 副①はっきりと ②すっかり, 完全に
- **clearly** 副①明らかに, はっきりと ②《返答に用いて》そのとおり
- **clerk** 名 事務員, 店員
- **climate** 名 気候, 風土, 環境
- **clover** 名 《植》シロツメクサ, クローバー
- **coast** 名 海岸, 沿岸 from coast to coast 大西洋岸から太平洋岸まで, 全米で 動 滑降する, ～の沿岸を航行する

Word List

- **code** 名 コード, 番号, 規準
- **coke** Coca-Cola の略, コカコーラ
- **cold cuts** コールドカット《ハムなどの冷肉》
- **colony** 名 植民[移民](地)
- **Columbus Day** コロンブス記念日
- **come out with** 〜を発表する, 市場に出す
- **comfortable** 形 快適な, 心地いい
- **commission** 名 手数料, 委託, 委任
- **common sense** 良識, 分別
- **commonly** 副 一般に, 通例
- **communicate** 動 ①知らせる, 連絡する ②理解し合う
- **communication** 名 ①コミュニケーション, 伝達, 連絡 ②通信機関
- **community** 名 ①団体, 共同社会, 地域社会 ②《the ‒》社会(一般), 世間 ③共有, 共同責任
- **commuter** 形 通勤(通学)の
- **compare** 動 ①〜を比較する, 〜を対照する ②〜にたとえる (**as**) **compared with [to]** 〜と比較して, 〜に比べれば
- **competition** 名 競争, 競合, コンペ
- **completely** 副 完全に, すっかり
- **complex** 形 入り組んだ, 複雑な
- **concern** 動 ①〜に関係する ②《受身形で》〜を心配する, 〜を気にする 名 ①関心事 ②関心, 心配 ③関係, 重要性
- **concert** 名 音楽[演奏]会
- **condiment** 名 調味料, 薬味
- **condition** 名 ①(健康)状態, 境遇 ②《-s》状況, 様子 ③条件 動 〜を適応させる, 〜を条件づける
- **conditioner** 名 調節器具, 冷房装置
- **conductor** 名 指導者, 案内者, 管理者, 指揮者, 車掌

- **cone** 名 錐, 円錐状の物, (アイスクリームの)コーン
- **confident** 形 自信のある, 自信に満ちた
- **Connecticut** 名 コネチカット《地名》
- **connection** 名 ①つながり, 関係 ②縁故 ③(電話の)通信
- **conservative** 形 ①保守的な, 保守主義の ②控えめな, 地味な
- **consider** 動 ①考慮する ②(〜と)みなす ③〜を気にかける, 思いやる
- **constitution** 名 ①憲法, 規約 ②構成, 構造
- **contemporary** 形 同時代の, 現代(風)の
- **contract** 名 契約(書), 協定 動 ①契約する ②縮小する
- **control** 動 ①〜を管理[支配]する ②〜を抑制する 名 ①管理, 支配(力) ②抑制
- **convenience** 名 便利(な物), 便宜
- **convenient** 形 便利な, 好都合な
- **conversation** 名 会話, 会談
- **convert** 動 変わ(え)る, 転向する, 改宗する
- **cookie** 名 クッキー
- **copy** 名 ①コピー ②(書籍の)一部, 冊 ③広告文 動 〜を写す, まねる
- **correct** 形 正しい, 適切な, りっぱな 動 (誤り)を訂正する, 〜を直す
- **cosmetic** 名 化粧品 形 美容の, 表面的な
- **cost** 名 ①値段, 費用 ②損失, 犠牲 動 (金, 費用)がかかる, 〜を要する
- **Costco** 名 コストコ《米の会員制スーパーマーケットチェーン》
- **costly** 形 高価な, ぜいたくな
- **costume** 名 衣装, 服装, 扮装, 仮装
- **counter** 名 (店の)売り台, カウンター, 計算器 形 反対の, 逆の
- **couple** 名 ①2つ, 対 ②夫婦, 一組, カップル ③2つ3つ, 数個

GET TO KNOW THE USA: ENJOY YOUR VISIT

- **coupon** 名クーポン, 優待券, 割引券
- **court** 名①中庭, コート ②法廷, 裁判所 ③宮廷, 宮殿 ④陳列場
- **cover** 動①～をおおう, ～を包む, ～を隠す ②～を扱う, ～にわたる ③代わりを務める 名おおい, カバー
- **crazy** 形①狂気の, ばかげた, 無茶な ②夢中の, 熱狂的な
- **cream** 名クリーム
- **create** 動～を創造する, ～を生み出す, ～を引き起こす
- **creation** 名①創造[物] ②ご馳走
- **credit** 名信用, 評判, 名声 store credit 返品と同額の買い物
- **crowded** 形混雑した, 満員の 動 crowd (群がる, 混雑する)の過去, 過去分詞
- **Cuban** 名形キューバ[人](の)
- **cuisine** 名料理, 料理法
- **cultural** 形文化の, 文化的な
- **cupcake** 名カップケーキ
- **customer** 名顧客
- **cut down on** ～を削減する, ～を軽減する

D

- **data** 名データ, 情報
- **day game** デイゲーム, 昼間行われる試合
- **Daylight Saving Time** 夏時間, サマータイム
- **deal** 動①～を分配する ②《 – with [in]》～を扱う 名①取引, 扱い ②(不特定の)量, 額
- **death** 名死,《the – 》終えん, 消滅
- **debit** 名借方, 負債, (口座からの)引き落とし額 **debit card** デビットカード, 銀行口座引き落としカード
- **decision** 名①決心 ②決定, 判決 ③決断(力)
- **declare** 動①～を宣言する ②～を断言する ③《税関で》～を申告する
- **deep-fried** 形油で揚げた
- **degree** 名①程度, 階級, 位, 身分 ②(温度・角度の)度
- **delay** 動～を遅らせる, ～を延期する 名遅延, 延期, 猶予
- **deli** 名デリカテッセン (=delicatessen)
- **deliver** 動①～を配達する, ～を伝える ②～を達成する, ～を果たす
- **delivery** 名①配達, 便 ②譲渡, 交付 ③出産
- **Democratic Party** 民主党《米の政党》
- **department** 名①部門, 課, 局, 担当分野 ②《D-》(米国・英国の)省 **department store** デパート
- **depend** 動《 – on [upon]》①～を頼る, ～をあてにする ②～による
- **describe** 動～を(言葉で)描写する, ～の特色を述べる, ～を説明する
- **design** 動～を設計する, ～を企てる 名デザイン, 設計(図)
- **desire** 動～を強く望む, ～を欲する 名欲望, 欲求, 願望
- **desperate** 形①絶望的な, 見込みのない ②ほしくてたまらない, 必死の
- **detail** 名①細部,《-s》詳細 ②《-s》個人情報 動～を詳しく述べる 形《-ed》詳細な
- **determine** 動①決定する[させる] ②～を正確に知る
- **develop** 動①発達する[させる] ②～を開発する
- **development** 名①発達, 発展 ②展開, 開発(地)
- **Devil's Night** ハロウィーンの前夜
- **dial** 動①電話をかける ②文字盤で示す 名①時計の文字盤 ②ダイヤル

WORD LIST

- **differently** 副異なって, 違って
- **digit** 名数字,（数字の）桁
- **dime** 名ダイム《米通貨・10セント》
- **dine** 動食事をする, ごちそうする
- **diner** 名①食事をする人 ②簡易食堂, 小食堂
- **direction** 名①方向, 方角, 道順, 説明書 ②《-s》指示 ③指導, 指揮
- **directly** 副①じかに ②まっすぐに ③ちょうど
- **directory** 名①住所氏名録, 建物案内板 ②訓令集, 規則書 形指揮［指導, 管理］の **directory assistance** 電話番号案内（サービス）
- **dirty** 形①汚い, よごれた ②卑劣な, 不正な ③無礼な, 軽蔑的な 動（〜を）汚す
- **disadvantage** 名不利な立場（条件）, 損失, 不便
- **discount** 名ディスカウント, 割引 動割引する, 軽視する 形安売りの
- **discovery** 名発見
- **discrimination** 名差別, 識別
- **discussion** 名討議, 討論
- **display** 動〜を展示する, 〜を示す 名展示, 陳列, 表出
- **distance** 名距離, 隔たり, 遠方
- **district** 名①地方, 地域 ②行政区
- **divide** 動分かれる［分ける］, 割れる［割る］
- **divorce** 動離婚する 名離婚, 分離
- **dome** 名ドーム, 屋根付き［室内］野球場
- **donation** 名寄付金, 献金
- **door-to-door** 形戸別の, ドアからドアへ
- **doorbell** 名玄関の呼び鈴［ベル］
- **double** 形①2倍の, 二重の ②対の 副①2倍に ②対で 動①2倍になる［する］ ②兼ねる
- **doubt** 名疑い, 不確かなこと 動〜を疑う **no doubt** きっと
- **down-home** 形家族的な, 素朴な
- **down jacket** ダウンジャケット
- **down side** マイナス面, 好ましくない点
- **downtown** 副商業地区［繁華街］へ 形商業地区［繁華街］の 名街の中心, 繁華街
- **Dr.** 名〜博士《医者に対して》〜先生
- **draw** 動①引く［引かれる］ ②〜を描く ③引き分けになる［する］
- **drawn** 動 draw（引く［引かれる］, 〜を描く）の過去分詞
- **dress code** 服装規定
- **driver** 名①運転手 ②（馬車の）御者
- **driver's license** 運転免許証
- **drugstore** 名薬局, ドラッグストア
- **dry town** 酒類の販売が禁止されている町
- **Dutch** 形オランダ［人］の 名オランダ人［語］
- **dying** 動 die（死ぬ, 消滅する）の現在分詞 形死にかかっている, 消えそうな **be dying for [to]〜** しきりに〜したがっている

E

- **e-mail** 名電子メール
- **earlier-than-usual** 形いつもより早い
- **early-bird** 形早朝の, 先駆けの
- **ease** 名安心, 気楽 **with ease** 簡単に 動〜を安心させる, 〜を楽にする, 〜をゆるめる
- **easily** 副①容易に, たやすく, 苦もなく ②気楽に
- **East Coast** 東海岸《米の大西洋岸北部地域》
- **Easter** 名《キリスト教》復活祭, イースター

Get to Know the USA: Enjoy Your Visit

- **easy-going** 形 のんきな, あくせくしない
- **eclectic** 形 ①取捨選択する ②折衷的な (主義の)
- **economic** 形 経済学の, 経済上の
- **economically** 副 経済的に, 節約して
- **education** 名 教育, 教養
- **effective** 形 効果的である, 有効である
- **effort** 名 努力 (の成果)
- **elderly** 形 かなり年配の, 初老の
- **election** 名 選挙, 投票
- **electricity** 名 電気 (代)
- **elsewhere** 副 どこかほかの所で (へ)
- **emergency** 名 非常時, 緊急時
  emergency room 救命救急センター
- **employee** 名 従業員, 使用人
- **encounter** 動 ~に(思いがけなく)出会う 名 遭遇, (思いがけない)出会い
- **encourage** 動 ①勇気づける, 励ます ②勧める
- **England** 名 ①イングランド ②英国
- **enjoy** 動 (特権など)を享受する
- **enjoyable** 形 愉快な, 楽しい
- **entertainment** 名 ①楽しみ, 娯楽 ②もてなし, 歓待
- **entire** 形 全体の, 完全な, 全くの
- **equal** 形 等しい, 均等な, 平等な 動 ~に匹敵する, 等しい
- **equality** 名 平等, 等しいこと
- **equally** 副 等しく, 平等に
- **equator** 名 《the –》赤道
- **estate** 名 不動産, 財産, 遺産, 地所, 土地
- **ethnic** 形 民族の, 人種的な, 異国の 名 少数派
- **Europe** 名 ヨーロッパ
- **European** 名 ヨーロッパ人 形 ヨーロッパ[人]の
- **everybody** 代 誰でも, 皆
- **everyday** 形 毎日の, 日々の
- **everyone** 代 誰でも, 皆
- **everything** 代 すべてのこと[もの], 何でも, 何もかも
- **everywhere** 副 どこにいても, いたるところに
- **evolve** 動 ①進化する, 発展する ②~を進化させる, ~を発展させる
- **exact** 形 正確な, 厳密な, きちょうめんな, ぴったりの
- **examine** 動 ~を試験する, ~を調査[検査]する, ~を診察する
- **excellent** 形 ①すぐれた, 優秀な, すばらしい ②(たいへん)結構です
- **except** 前 ~を除いて, ~のほかは except for ~ ~を除いて, ~がなければ 接 ~ということを除いて
- **exercise** 名 ①運動, 体操 ②練習 動 運動, 練習する
- **exhibition** 名 展示会, 見本市, エキシビション
- **exist** 動 存在する, 生存する, ある
- **exit** 名 出口, 退去 動 退出する, 退去する
- **expect** 動 ~を予期[予測]する, (当然のこととして)~を期待する
- **expense** 名 ①出費, 費用 ②犠牲, 代価
- **experimental** 形 実験の, 試験的な
- **expiration** 名 期限切れ, 満了, 満期 expiration date 有効期限
- **express** 動 ~を表現する, ~を述べる 形 ①明白な ②急行の 名 速達便, 急行列車 副 速達で, 急行で
- **expression** 名 ①表現, 表示, 表情 ②言い回し, 語句
- **extended** 形 延長した, 広範な
- **extra** 形 余分の, 臨時の 名 ①余分なもの ②エキストラ 副 余分に

Word List

F

- **fair** 形①正しい, 公平[正当]な ②快晴の ③色白の, 金髪の ④かなりの 副①公平に, きれいに ②みごとに
- **fairly** 副①公平に ②かなり, 相当に
- **fairness** 名公平さ, 公明正大さ
- **fall** 動①(記念日などが〜(曜)日に)あたる ②fall in [to] 〜に分類される ③(ある状態に)急に陥る
- **fancy** 名①幻想, 空想 ②想像力 形①装飾的な, みごとな ②法外な, 高級な 動①〜を心に描く, 〜と考える ②〜を好む, 〜に引かれる
- **faraway** 形遠い, 遠方の
- **fare** 名運賃, 料金
- **fashion** 名①流行, 方法, はやり ②流行のもの(特に服装)
- **fashionable** 形流行の, おしゃれな
- **fast-food** 形ファーストフード専門の, 即席の
- **Father's Day** 父の日
- **feature** 名①特徴, 特色 ②顔の一部,《-s》顔立ち ③(ラジオ・テレビ・新聞などの)特集 動①〜の特徴になる ②〜を呼び物にする 形《-ed》呼び物の
- **federal** 形連邦政府の, 連邦の **federal law** 名連邦法
- **fee** 名謝礼, 料金 動謝礼を払う
- **fiddle** 動いじくる, もてあそぶ, みだりに変える
- **figure** 名①人(物)の姿, 形 ②図(形), 象徴 ③数字 動①〜を描写する, 〜を想像する ②〜を計算する ③目立つ
- **Filipino** 名フィリピン人
- **fill in** 〜に記入する
- **filling** 形食べ応えのある 名(サンドイッチなどの)中身
- **final** 形最後の, 決定的な 名①最後のもの ②《-s》決勝戦, 最終試験
- **financial** 形①財務上の, 金融上の, 金銭上の ②金融関係者の
- **finger-lickin'** 形指についた残りまでなめたくなるほど
- **fire-fighter** 名消防士
- **firework** 名花火
- **first-class** 形一流の, (乗り物の)一等,《郵便》第1種の
- **fitting** 形適切な, ふさわしい
- **flick** 名①軽く打つこと, はじくこと ②ピシッという音 ③《俗》映画(館) 動〜を軽く打つ, ピシッとはじく
- **flight** 飛ぶこと, 飛行, (飛行機の)フライト
- **Florida** 名フロリダ《米国の州》
- **flow** 動流れ出る, あふれる 名流出, 流ちょう(なこと), 流れ
- **following** 名①支持(賛同)者, 随行者 ②次に述べるもの
- **football** 名《英》サッカー,《米》アメリカンフットボール
- **for a while** 少しの間, しばらく
- **force** 名力, 勢い 動〜に強制する, 力づくで〜する
- **foreigner** 名外国人, 外国製品
- **form** 名①形, 形式 ②書式 動〜を形づくる
- **formal** 形正式の, 公式の, 形式的な, 格式ばった
- **formerly** 副元は, 以前は
- **freedom** 名①自由 ②束縛がないこと ③政治的独立
- **freelance** 名フリーランサー 形フリーランスの, 自由契約の
- **French** 形フランス(人[語])の 名フランス語,《the -》フランス人
- **frequently** 副頻繁に, しばしば
- **fried** 形油で揚げた, フライ料理の
- **friendliness** 名友情, 好意
- **friendly** 形親しみのある, 親切な, 友情のこもった 副友好的に, 親切に
- **funeral** 名葬式, 葬列 形葬式の
- **furniture** 名家具, 備品, 調度

GET TO KNOW THE USA: ENJOY YOUR VISIT

- **further** 形いっそう遠い, その上の, なおいっそうの 副いっそう遠く, その上に, もっと 動~を促進する

G

- **gardener** 名庭師, 園芸家
- **gas** 名①ガス, 気体 ②ガソリン 動~をガスにさらす
- **gather** 動①集まる[集める] ②生じる, 増す ③~を推測する
- **gay** 形①同性愛の ②快活な, 陽気な, 派手な **gay marriage** 同性婚 名同性愛者
- **gayness** 名①陽気 ②ゲイであること
- **general** 形①全体の, 一般の, 普通の ②おおよその **in a general way** 一般的に 名大将, 将軍
- **generalize** 動~を一般化する, 一般的に言う, 法則化する
- **generally** 副①一般に, だいたい ②たいてい
- **generation** 動世代, 同時代の人
- **German** 形ドイツの, ドイツ人の, ドイツ語の 名ドイツ人, ドイツ語
- **Germany** 名ドイツ
- **get a dirty look** 嫌な顔をされる
- **get along** (何とか)やっていく, うまくいく
- **get around** あちこちに移動する, 動き回る
- **get in the way of** ~を邪魔[妨害]する, ~の邪魔[障害]になる
- **get lost** 見失う, 道に迷う
- **gift** 名①贈り物 ②(天賦の)才能 動~を授ける
- **Gold Rush** ゴールドラッシュ《1849年カリフォルニアが有名》
- **golden** 副①金色の ②金製の ③貴重な

- **gotten** 動 get (~を得る)の過去分詞
- **gourmet** 名グルメ, 美食家 形グルメな, グルメ向きの
- **government** 名政治, 政府, 支配
- **grade** 名学年, 等級, グレード 動~を格づけする
- **graduate school** 大学院
- **grant** 動①~を許可する, ~を承諾する ②~を授与する, ~を譲渡する ③~を(なるほどと)認める 名①認可, 承諾 ②授与, 補助[金]
- **grateful** 形感謝する, ありがたく思う
- **Great Depression** 世界大恐慌《1929年に米でおこる》
- **greatly** 副大いに
- **Greek** 形ギリシャ[人]の, ギリシャ語の 名ギリシャ人, ギリシャ語
- **green stuff** ①野菜類, 青物 ②ドル札
- **greet** 動①(人)にあいさつする ②~を(喜んで)迎える 名《-ing》あいさつ(の言葉), あいさつ(状)
- **ground level** 地表面《英》1階
- **guest** 名客, ゲスト

H

- **habit** 名習慣, 癖, 気質
- **hall** 名公会堂, ホール, 大広間
- **Halloween** 名ハロウィーン
- **ham** 名ハム
- **hamburger** 名ハンバーガー
- **handful** 一握り, 少量の
- **handicapped** 形身体に障害のある, ハンディキャップのある
- **handsome** 形端正な(顔立ちの), りっぱな, (男性が)ハンサムな
- **hang** 動かかる[かける], ~をつるす, ぶら下がる **hang out** うろつく,

Word List

ブラブラする 名 かかり具合
- **Hanukkah** 名 ハヌカー《ユダヤ教の清めの祭り》
- **hard-boiled** 形 ①非情な、ハードボイルドな ②固ゆでの
- **hardware** 名 ①金物類(製品) ②(コンピュータの)ハードウェア
- **have one's hair done** 散髪してもらう
- **Hawaii** 名 ハワイ《地名》
- **headquarters** 名 本部、司令部、本署
- **health check** 検診、健康診断
- **health-food** 形 健康食品の
- **health insurance** 医療保険、健康保険
- **healthy** 形 健康な、健全な、健康によい
- **heat** 名 ①熱、暑さ ②熱気、熱意、激情 動 (~を)熱する、暖める
- **heaven** 名 ①天国 ②天国のようなところ[状態]、楽園
- **Hebrew** 名 ヘブライ人[語] 形 ヘブライ人[語・文字・文化]の
- **helpful** 形 役に立つ、参考になる
- **here and there** あちこちで
- **hi-tech** 形 ハイテクな[の]
- **high-chair** 名 子供用の背の高いイス
- **high-class** 形 高級な、一流の
- **hippie movement** ヒッピー運動《米で1960年代から70年代に起こった》
- **hire** 動 ~を雇う、~を賃借りする 名 雇用、賃借り、使用料
- **Hispanic** 名 ラテンアメリカ系の人、スペイン語を話す人 形 ラテンアメリカ系の、スペイン人[語]の
- **hobby** 名 趣味、得意なこと
- **Home Depot** ホーム・ディーポ《全米ホームセンターチェーン》
- **homework** 名 宿題、予習
- **honey-roasted peanuts** はちみつでローストしたピーナッツ
- **honor** 名 ①名誉、光栄、信用 ②節操、自尊心 動 ~を尊敬する、~に栄誉を与える
- **hospitality** 名 歓待、温かいもてなし
- **host** 名 ①客をもてなす主人 ②(テレビなどの)司会者
- **hot dog** ホットドック
- **hot-dog stand** ホットドック売りの屋台
- **housework** 名 家事
- **however** 副 たとえ~でも 接 けれども、だが
- **huge** 形 巨大な、ばくだいな
- **humid** 形 湿った、むしむしする
- **humidity** 名 湿度、湿気
- **hunger** 名 ①空腹、飢え ②(~の)欲 動 ①飢える ②熱望する
- **hunt** 動 ~を狩る、狩りをする、~を捜し求める 名 狩り、追跡
- **hunter** 名 ①狩りをする人 ②猟馬、猟犬、捜し求める人

I

- **I.D.** 名 身分証明書、身分を証明できるもの
- **icing** 名 アイシング、糖衣(砂糖で作ってケーキにかける)
- **icy** 形 氷の(多い)、氷のように冷たい、氷で覆われた
- **ideal** 名 理想、目標 形 理想的な
- **identification** 名 ①身元確認 ②同一であることの確認
- **IGA** 名 IGA《全米スーパーマーケットチェーン》
- **immigration** 名 ①移民局、入国管理 ②移住、入植 immigration law

GET TO KNOW THE USA: ENJOY YOUR VISIT

移民法

- **importantly** 副重大に, もったいぶって, 重要なことだが
- **impression** 名①印象, 感想 ②感動
- **in any case** ともかく, どんな場合でも
- **include** 動~を含む, ~を勘定に入れる
- **increase** 動増加[増強]する[させる] 名増加(量), 増大
- **indeed** 副実際, 本当に, 《強意》全く 間本当に, まさか
- **Independence Day** 独立記念日
- **Indian** 名①インド人 ②(アメリカ)インディアン 形①インドの, インド人の ②(アメリカ)インディアンの
- **indicator** 名指示する人, 指示器, 標識
- **individual** 形独立した, 個性的な, 個々の 名①個人, 個体 ②人
- **industrialization** 名工業化, 産業化
- **inexpensive** 形費用のかからない, 安い, あまり高価でない
- **influence** 名影響, 勢力 動~に影響をおよぼす
- **initial** 形最初の, 初めの 名頭文字 動頭文字で署名する
- **in order to~** ~するために
- **input** 動入力する 名入力, 投入
- **insecure** 形不安定な, 心細い
- **insight** 名洞察, 真相, 見識
- **instance** 名①例 ②場合, 事実 ③請求, 依頼 動~を例としてあげる
- **instant** 形即時の, 緊急の, 即席の 名瞬間, 寸時
- **instead** 副その代わりに instead of~ ~の代わりに, ~をしないで
- **insurance** 名保険
- **insure** 動①~に保険をかける ②

~を保証する, ~を請け合う
- **in turn** ①順に, 次々に ②その結果
- **invitation** 名招待(状), 案内(状)
- **Ireland** 名アイルランド
- **Irises** 名アイリス《花, ゴッホの有名な作品名》
- **Irish** 形アイルランド[人]の
- **Irish American** アイルランド系アメリカ人
- **issue** 名①問題, 論点 ②発行物 ③出口, 流出 動①(~から)出る, 生じる ②~を発行する
- **Italian** 名イタリア人[語] 形イタリア(人[語])の
- **itself** 代それ自体, それ自身

J

- **Japan** 名日本
- **Japanese** 名日本人(語) 形日本の, 日本製の, 日本人(語)の
- **jeans** 名ジーンズ, ジーパン
- **Jew** 名ユダヤ人, ユダヤ教徒
- **Jewish** 形ユダヤ人の, ユダヤ教の
- **joke** 名冗談, ジョーク 動冗談を言う, ふざける, からかう
- **Judaism** 名ユダヤ教
- **junk food** ジャンクフード《栄養価の低いスナック菓子》

K

- **Kentucky Fried Chicken** ケンタッキー・フライド・チキン
- **ketchup** 名ケチャップ
- **keyboard** 名(ピアノなどの)鍵盤, キーボード
- **kick around** ~のあちこち動き回る, うろつく

Word List

- **kiddie** 名子供
- **kill time** 時間[暇]をつぶす
- **kin** 名家族, 親類
- **kindness** 名親切(な行為), 優しさ
- **kiss** 名キス 動~にキスする
- **Kmart** 名Kマート《米のスーパーマーケットチェーン》
- **Korean** 形朝鮮[韓国]の, 朝鮮[韓国]人[語]の 名朝鮮[韓国]人
- **Kwanzaa** 名クワンザ《アフリカ系アメリカ人の祭り》

L

- **label** 名標札, ラベル
- **labor** 名労働, 骨折り 動①働く, 努力する, 骨折る ②苦しむ, 悩む
- **Labor Day** 労働者の日
- **lack** 動(~が)不足している, 欠けている 名不足, 欠乏
- **landlord** 名①(男の)家主, 地主 ②パブの主人
- **laptop** 名ラップトップコンピュータ, ノート型パソコン 形ひざのせ型の
- **largely** 副大いに, 主として
- **Latin America** ラテンアメリカ《中南米諸国の総称》
- **Latino** 名形ラテンアメリカ系住民(の)
- **lawn** 名芝生
- **lawyer** 名弁護士, 法律家
- **lay** 動①~を置く, ~を横たえる, ~を敷く ②~を整える ③卵を産む ④lie(横たわる, (ある状態に)ある)の過去
- **lazy** 形怠惰な, 無精な
- **league** 名①同盟, 連盟 ②《スポーツ》競技連盟
- **lease** 名賃貸, リース 動~を賃貸しする, 賃借りする

- **least** 形一番小さい, 最も少ない 副一番小さく, 最も少なく 名最小[少] **at least** 少なくとも, いずれにしても
- **led** 動lead(~を導く)の過去, 過去分詞
- **legal** 形法律(上)の, 正当な
- **length** 名長さ, 縦, たけ, 距離
- **less** 形~より小さい[少ない], 劣った 副~より少なく, ~ほどでなく 名より少ない数[量・額]
- **level** 名①水平, 平面 ②水準 形水平の, 平たい ②同等[同位]の 動①~を水平にする ②~を平等にする
- **liberal** 形①自由主義の, 進歩的な ②気前のよい 名自由主義者
- **license** 名免許, ライセンス 動(法的機関が)許可する, 免許を与える
- **lifestyle** 名ライフスタイル, 生活様式
- **likely** 形①ありそうな, ~しそうな ②適当な 副たぶん, おそらく
- **limit** 名限界, 《-s》範囲, 境界 動~を制限[限定]する 形《-ed》限られた, 不足している
- **limousine** 名リムジン《送迎用の大型の乗用車》
- **Lincoln** 名①リンカーン《人名》 ②リンカーン《米製の車の名前》
- **liquor** 名(強い)酒, 蒸留酒 **liquor license** リカーライセンス《酒を販売できる許可》
- **list** 名名簿, 目録, 一覧表 動~を名簿[目録]に記入する
- **Little Seoul** リトル・ソウル《韓国人が集まって暮らす地区の愛称》
- **live on** ①~で生活を立てる ②存在し続ける
- **local paper** 地方紙(新聞)
- **long-distance** 形長距離の, 遠く離れた
- **long for** ~を切望する
- **look up** ~を調べる

GET TO KNOW THE USA: ENJOY YOUR VISIT

- **Los Angeles** ロサンゼルス《地名》
- **lot** 名一区画,用地 **parking lot** 駐車場
- **loudly** 副大声で,騒がしく
- **lover** 名①愛人,恋人 ②愛好者
- **low-cost** 形低コストの,廉価な
- **lunar** 形月の,月面の **lunar calendar** 旧暦,太陰暦
- **lunch time** 昼食時間
- **luxury** 形豪華な,高級な,贅沢な 名豪華さ,贅沢(品)

M

- **made up of** 《be –》~で構成されている
- **mail-order** 名通信販売,通販 形通販の
- **mailbox** 名郵便箱(受け)
- **mailmen** 名mailman(郵便配達人)の複数
- **main** 形①主な,主要な ②力いっぱいの 名①力,勢力 ②主要部
- **major** 形①大きいほうの,主な,一流の ②年長[古参]の 名①陸軍少佐 ②専攻科目 動~を専攻する
- **Major League** メジャー・リーグ《野球》
- **majority** 名①大多数,過半数 ②成年
- **maker** 名製造業者
- **mall** 名ショッピングモール,商店街
- **manager** 名経営者,支配人,支店長,部長
- **Manhattan** 名マンハッタン《地名》
- **manner** 名①方法,やり方 ②態度,様子 ③《-s》行儀,作法,生活様式
- **manufacturer** 名製造業者,メーカー

- **Mapquest** 名マップクエスト《地図検索のインターネットサイト》
- **mark** 名①印,記号,跡 ②点数 ③特色 動①~に印[記号]をつける ②採点する ③~を目立たせる,(行事を)祝う
- **marriage** 名結婚(生活[式])
- **marry** 動(~と)結婚する
- **married** 形結婚している
- **Martin Luther King Jr.** マーティン・ルーサー・キング・ジュニア《黒人の人権活動家》
- **mass** 名①固まり,(密集した)集まり ②多数,多量 ③《the –》大衆 動~を一団にする,集める,固まる
- **Massachusetts** 名マサチューセッツ《地名》
- **masterpiece** 名傑作,名作,代表作
- **material** 形①物質の,肉体的な ②不可欠な,重要な 名①材料,原料 ②物質,物 ③資料,データ
- **matinee** 名マチネ《演劇・音楽などの昼の興行》
- **Maulana Ron Karenga** マウラナ・カレンガ博士《カリフォルニア州立大学教授。1966年にクワンザ(Kwanzaa)を提唱》
- **Mayflower** 名メイフワラー号《ピルグリムファーザーが乗船していた船の名》
- **mayonnaise** 名マヨネーズ
- **McDonald's** 名マクドナルド
- **means** 名手段,方法 **by any means** 《not –》決して~でない
- **medical** 形①医学[医療]の ②内科の 名医学生
- **mega** 形大きい,巨大な **mega store** 大型店,メガストア
- **melting pot** るつぼ
- **membership** 名会員,会員資格
- **Memorial Day** 戦没者記念日,メモリアルデー

Word List

- **memory** 名記憶(力), 思い出
- **menorah** 名9本枝の燭台《ユダヤ教のハヌカー祭で使う》
- **mention** 動~について述べる, 言及する 名言及, 陳述
- **menu** 名メニュー, 献立表
- **merry** 形陽気な, 愉快な, 快活な
- **messenger** 名使者, (伝言・小包などの)配達人, 伝達者
- **meter** 名①メートル《長さの単位》 ②計量器, 計量する人
- **method** 名①方法, 手段 ②秩序, 体系
- **metric** 形メートル(法)の 名測定基準
- **Metro North** メトロノース《ニューヨーク近郊都市を結ぶ列車》
- **Metropolitan Museum of Art** メトロポリタン・ミュージアム《Metは略称》
- **Mexican** 名形メキシコ(の), メキシコ人(の)
- **Mexican War** メキシコ戦争《1846–48, メキシコとアメリカ間の戦争》
- **middle** 名中間, 最中 形中間の, 中央の middle school 中学校
- **Middle East** 中東《リビアからアフガニスタンに及ぶ諸国の総称》
- **Middle-Eastern** 形中東の
- **middle-aged** 形中高年の
- **midnight** 名真夜中, 夜の12時, 暗黒 形真夜中の, 真っ暗な
- **mile** 名①マイル《長さの単位。1,609m》②《-s》かなりの距離
- **mileage** 名①総マイル数, マイレッジ ②マイル当たり料金
- **military** 形軍隊[軍人]の, 軍事の 名《the –》軍, 軍部
- **mind** 名①心, 精神 ②知性 with ~in mind ~を念頭において 動①~を嫌だと思う ②~に気をつける, ~を用心する
- **mix** 動①混ざる[混ぜる] ②~を一緒にする 名混合(物)
- **mobile** 形移動しやすい, 携帯できる 名携帯電話
- **mobility** 名可動性, 動きやすさ
- **modern dance** モダンダンス
- **money order** 送金(郵便)為替
- **monster** 名怪物
- **mostly** 副主として, 多くは, ほとんど
- **Mother's Day** 母の日
- **movement** 名①動き, 運動 ②《-s》行動 ③引越し ④変動
- **murder** 名人殺し, 殺害, 殺人事件 動~を殺す
- **museum** 名博物館, 美術館
- **musical** 形音楽の 名ミュージカル
- **Muslim** 名イスラム教徒 形イスラム教の
- **mustard** 名マスタード

N

- **nail** 名①つめ ②くぎ, びょう 動~にくぎを打つ, ~をくぎづけにする
- **nanny** 名子守り, ベビーシッター
- **nation** 名国, 国家, 《the –》国民
- **national** 形国家[国民]の, 全国の
- **National League** ナショナルリーグ, ナ・リーグ《野球》
- **national spirit** 国民精神
- **native** 形①出生(地)の, 自国の ②(~に)固有の, 生まれつきの, 天然の 名(~)生まれの人
- **Native American** アメリカ先住民(の), ネイティブ・アメリカン(の)
- **Native Hawaiian** ハワイ先住民(の)

139

Get to Know the USA: Enjoy Your Visit

- **naturally** 副 生まれつき, 自然に, 当然のことながら
- **nearly** 副 ①近くに, 親しく ②ほとんど, あやうく
- **neat** 形 きちんとした, きれいな
- **necessarily** 副 《否定語を伴って》必ずしも～でない, やむを得ず
- **necessary** 形 必要な, 必然の 名 《-s》必需品, 必需品
- **neither** 形 どちらの～も…でない 代 （2者のうち）どちらも～でない 副 《否定文に続いて》～も…しない
- **Net** 名 《the -》インターネット
- **New Milford** ニューミルフォード《地名》
- **New Year's Day** 正月
- **New York** ニューヨーク《地名》
- **New York City** ニューヨーク市《地名》
- **New Yorker** ニューヨークの人
- **newspaper** 名 新聞（紙）
- **next to nothing** ほとんどなきに等しい, ただも同然で
- **nickel** 名 5セント《米通貨》
- **night-time game** ナイトゲーム《野球》
- **nineteenth** 名 《通例the -》第19番目（の人[物]）, 19日 形 《通例the-》第19番目の
- **no longer** もはや～でない
- **no matter** ～を問わず
- **no-smoking** 形 禁煙の
- **nobody** 代 誰も[1人も]～ない 名 とるに足らない人
- **non-American** 名 アメリカ市民（人）でない人
- **non-profit** 形 非営利の
- **non-religious** 形 非宗教の
- **non-smoking** 形 禁煙の
- **non-food** 形 食品以外の
- **noodle** 名 麺類, ヌードル

- **normal** 形 普通の, 平常の, 標準的な 名 平常, 標準, 典型
- **normally** 副 普通は, 通常は
- **northeast** 名形 ①北東（の）, 北東部（の） ②《N-》（米国の）北東部 副 北東に（へ）
- **northern** 形 北の, 北向きの, 北からの
- **not-so-good** 形 そんなに良くない
- **notebook** 名 ノート, 手帳
- **notebook computer** ノート型パソコン
- **notice** 名 ①注意 ②通知 ③公告 動 ①～に気づく, ～を認める ②～に通告する
- **nowadays** 副 この頃は, 現在では
- **nowhere** 副 どこにも～ない **in the middle of nowhere** 人里離れた
- **nurse** 名 ①看護師［人］ ②乳母 動 ①～を看病する ②～をあやす
- **nutcracker** 名 クルミ割り器 **The Nutcracker** くるみ割人形《バレエの演目》

O

- **occasion** 名 ①場合, 折 ②機会, 好機 ③理由, 根拠
- **occupancy** 名 占有, 使用
- **odd** 形 ①奇妙な ②奇数の ③（一対のうちの）片方の
- **off-season** 形 季節外れの, シーズンオフの
- **offer** 動 （～を）申し出る, （～を）申し込む, （～を）提供する 名 提案, 提供
- **Office Max** オフィス・マックス《全米の文房具販売チェーン》
- **office supply** オフィス用品
- **Ohio** 名 オハイオ《地名》
- **okay** 形 《許可, 同意, 満足などを表

WORD LIST

して》よろしい, 正しい 名許可, 承認
- **old-style** 形旧式の, 伝統的な
- **old saying** ことわざ, いい習わし
- **one by one** ひとつずつ
- **online** 名オンライン 形オンラインの, ネットワーク上の 副オンラインで
- **on the other hand** 他方では, 逆に
- **on the way** 途中で
- **on time** 時間通りに
- **open-air** 名形野外[戸外] (での)
- **opera** 名歌劇, オペラ
- **operate** 動①(機械などが)動く, ~を運転する, ~を管理する ②作用する ③手術する ④経営[運営]する
- **operator** 名オペレーター, 交換手, 操作する人
- **opportunity** 名好機, 適当な時期[状況]
- **opposite** 形反対の, 向こう側の 前~の向こう側に 名反対の人[物]
- **ordinary** 形①普通の, 通常の ②並の, 平凡な
- **organization** 名①組織(化), 編成, 団体, 機関 ②有機体, 生物
- **original** 形①始めの, 元の, 本来の ②独創的な 名原型, 原文
- **originally** 副最初は, そもそもは
- **outlet** 名①出口 ②(電気の)コンセント ②直販店, 販路, アウトレット
- **out of place** 場違いの, 不適当の
- **over and over** 何度も繰り返して
- **overseas** 形海外の, 外国への 副海外に 名外国
- **owner** 名持ち主, オーナー

P

- **Pacific Islander** 太平洋諸島の人
- **package** 名包み, 小包, パッケージ 動~を包装する, ~を荷造りする 形(計画・提案などの)一括の
- **packed** 形混んだ, 満員の
- **pancake** 名パンケーキ
- **parade** 名パレード, 行列
- **paradox** 名パラドックス, 逆説, 矛盾した(ように見える)こと
- **participation** 名参加, 加入
- **particular** 形①特別の, 特定の ②詳細な ③各自の, 特有の 名事項, 細部, 《-s》詳細 **in particular** 特に, とりわけ
- **particularly** 副特に, とりわけ
- **partner** 名配偶者, 仲間, 同僚 動(パートナーとして)~と組む[組ませる]
- **passenger** 名乗客, 旅客
- **Passover** 名(ユダヤ教の)過越しの祭り
- **passport** 名パスポート, (通行)許可証
- **past** 形過去の, この前の 名過去(の出来事) 前(時間が)~を過ぎて, ~を越して 副通り越して, 過ぎて
- **pasta** 名パスタ
- **pastel** 形パステルカラーの, パステル画の
- **pastrami** 名パストラミ
- **patron** 名後援者, パトロン
- **pattern** 名①柄, 型, 模様 ②手本, 模範 動①~を手本にする ②~に模様をつける
- **pavement** 名舗道
- **pay** 動~を払う, ~に報いる 名給料, 報い **pay phone** 公衆電話
- **payment** 名支払い
- **pedicab** 名人を乗せて走る三輪自転車

GET TO KNOW THE USA: ENJOY YOUR VISIT

- **peg** 動①~にくぎを打つ,固定する,安定させる ②分類する
- **pennant** 名ペナント,優勝旗
- **penny** 名①ペニー,ペンス《英国の貨幣単位。1/100ポンド》②《否定文で》小銭,びた一文 ③《米・カナダ》1セント銅貨
- **percentage** 名パーセンテージ,割合,比率
- **perfectly** 副完全に,申し分なく
- **performance** 名①実行,行為 ②成績,できばえ ③演劇,演奏
- **performing arts** 舞台(公演)芸術
- **perhaps** 副たぶん,ことによると
- **period** 名期,期間,時代 形時代物の
- **personal** 形①個人の ②本人自らの ③容姿の **personal check** 個人小切手
- **Philippine** 名フィリピン《地名》,フィリピン人
- **phone chain** 電話の連絡網
- **physical** 形①物質の,物理学の,自然科学の ②身体の,肉体の
- **picnic** 名ピクニック
- **pickup service** 集荷サービス,送迎サービス
- **Pilgrims** 名巡礼者,初期入植者
- **pizza** 名ピザ
- **plain** 形①明白な,はっきりした ②簡素な ③平らな ④あっさりした
- **plate** 名①(浅い)皿,1皿の料理 ②金属板,標札
- **player** 名①競技者,選手,演奏者,俳優 ②演奏装置
- **pleasant** 形①(物事が)楽しい,心地よい ②快活な,愛想のよい
- **pleasure** 名喜び,楽しみ,満足,娯楽 動楽しむ[楽しませる]
- **Plymouth** 名プリマス《地名》
- **Pole** 名①ポーランド人(=Polish)

- **policy** 名①政策,方針,手段 ②保険証券
- **polite** 形ていねいな,礼儀正しい,洗練された
- **politically** 副政治上,政治的に
- **politics** 名政治(学),政策
- **popcorn** 名ポップコーン
- **popularity** 名人気,流行
- **population** 名人口,住民(数)
- **position** 名①位置,場所 ②地位,身分,職 ③立場,状況
- **possible** 形可能な,あり[起こり]得る
- **post** 動掲示する
- **postal** 形郵便の,郵送の
- **postcard** 名(絵)はがき
- **pound** 名①ポンド《英国の通貨単位。記号£》②ポンド《重量の単位。453.6g》
- **powerful** 形力強い,実力のある,影響力のある
- **practical** 形実際的な,実用的な,役に立つ
- **prank** 名いたずら,悪ふざけ
- **prefecture** 名県,府
- **prefer** 動~のほうを好む,~のほうがよいと思う
- **preference** 名好きであること,好み
- **prepaid** 形プリペイドの,前払いの
- **presence** 名①存在(すること),いること ②そば,近接
- **presidential** 形大統領の
- **Presidents' Day** ワシントン大統領誕生記念日
- **pretzel** 名プレッツェル
- **price** 名①値段,代価,代償 ②《-s》物価,相場
- **priority** 名優先順位,より重要であること,プライオリティ
- **priority mail** 優先扱い郵便物

Word List

- **privacy** 名 (干渉されない) 自由な生活, プライバシー
- **private** 形 ①私的な, 個人の ②民間の ③内密の, 人里離れた
- **privately** 副 内密に, 非公式に, 個人的に
- **probably** 副 たぶん, おそらく
- **process** 名 ①過程, 経過, 進行 ②手順, 方法, 製法, 加工
- **produce** 名 農産物, 生鮮食品
- **product** 名 ①製品, 産物 ②成果, 結果
- **profession** 名 職業, 専門職
- **professor** 名 教授, 師匠
- **profit** 名 利益, 利潤, ため 動 (物事が) (人) のためになる, 役立つ
- **project** 名 計画, 企画, 事業
- **prompt** 動 促す, 鼓舞する, 促して~させる 形 迅速な, 機敏な 名 促進
- **pronunciation** 名 発音
- **proper** 形 ①適した, 適切な, 正しい ②固有の
- **property** 名 ①財産, 所有物 [地] ②性質, 属性 property tax 固定資産税
- **provide** 動 ~に…を供給する, 用意する, (~に) 備える 《-ed》接 ~という条件で, もし~ならば
- **PTA** 略 ピーティーエー (=Parent-Teacher Association)
- **publication** 名 出版 (物), 発行, 発表
- **public grant** 公の助成金
- **Puerto Rican** プエルトリコ [人] (の)
- **purchase** 動 ~を購入する, ~を獲得する 名 購入 (物), 仕入れ, 獲得
- **put thought into** 考える, 工夫する
- **puzzle** 動 ~を迷わせる, 当惑する [させる] 名 ①難問, 当惑 ②パズル

Q

- **quarter** 名 ①4分の1, 15分 ②25セント《米通貨。4分の1ドル》動 ~を4等分する
- **quickly** 副 敏速に, 急いで
- **quite a bit** かなりたくさんの
- **quite a few** 相当数の, かなりの数の

R

- **racial** 形 人種の, 民族の
- **rack** 名 ラック, 網棚, 格子棚 動《be -ed》苦しむ
- **rail** 名 ①横木, 手すり ②レール, 鉄道
- **railroad** 名 鉄道, 路線
- **raise** 動 ①~を上げる [高める] ②~を起こす ③~を育てる 名 高める [上げる] こと, 昇給 形《-ed》高くした
- **range** 名 列, 連なり, 範囲 動 ①並ぶ [並べる] ②~に及ぶ
- **rapidly** 副 速く, 急速に, 素早く, 迅速に
- **rate** 名 ①割合, 率 ②相場, 料金 動 ①~を見積もる, 評価する [される] ②~に等級をつける
- **rather** 副 ①むしろ, かえって ②いくぶん, やや would rather むしろ~したい [するほうがよい]
- **reach out** ①手を伸ばす ②接触する, 連絡しようとする
- **real estate** 不動産 real estate agency 不動産業者
- **realize** 動 ①~を理解する, ~を実現する ②適当な, (値段が) 相応する
- **rear** 名 後ろ, 背後 形 後ろの 動 ①~を上げる [立てる] ②~を育てる
- **reasonable** 形 ①筋の通った, 分別のある ②適当な, (値段が) 相応な
- **reasonably** 副 分別よく, 賢明に,

Get to Know the USA: Enjoy Your Visit

適当に，かなり
- **receipt** 名 受領書，受け取ること
  gift receipt 贈り物を渡す相手用のレシート
- **recent** 形 近頃の，近代の
- **recently** 副 ついこのあいだ，近頃
- **reception** 名 ①もてなし，接待，宴会，受付 ②評判 ③電波の(受信)状態
- **recognize** 動 ～を認める，～を認識[承認]する，思い出す
- **recommend** 動 ①～を推薦する ②～を勧告する，忠告する
- **record** 名 記録，登録，履歴 動 ～を記録[登録]する，録音[画]する
- **Red Lobster** レッドロブスター《米の外食チェーン店》
- **red-letter** 形 赤文字の，特筆すべき，記念の
- **reduce** 動 ①～を減じる ②～をしいて…させる，～を…の状態にする 形 《-ed》減少した，割引した
- **reflect** 動 映る，反響する，反射する，再現する
- **regardless** 形 無頓着な，注意しない 副 それにもかかわらず，それでも
  regardless of ～に関係なく
- **region** 名 ①地方，地域 ②範囲
- **register** 動 登録する，署名する，書留にする 名 一覧表，記録
- **registered mail** 書留郵便
- **regular** 形 ①規則的な，秩序のある ②定期的な，通常の，習慣的な 名 常連
- **regular-priced** 形 定価の
- **relative** 形 関係のある，相対的な 名 親戚，同族
- **relax** 動 くつろがせる[くつろぐ]，ゆるめる
- **religion** 名 宗教，～教，信条
- **religious** 形 ①宗教の ②信心深い
- **remind** 動 ～に…を思い出させる
- **rent** 動 ～を賃借りする 名 使用料，賃貸料

- **rental** 形 賃貸の，レンタルの 名 賃貸料，賃借
- **repeat** 動 (～を)繰り返す 名 繰り返し，反復，再演
- **replace** 動 ①～を取り替える，～に取って代わる ②元に戻す
- **reply** 動 答える，返事をする，応答する 名 答え，返事，応答
- **represent** 動 ①～を表現する ②～を意味する ③～を代表する ④～に相当する
- **representative** 名 ①代表(者) ②代議士，国会議員
- **Republican Party** 共和党《米の政党》
- **request** 名 願い，要求(物)，需要 動 ～を求める，～を申し込む
- **require** 動 ①～を必要とする，～を要する ②～を命じる，～を請求する
- **reservation** 名 ①留保，制限 ②予約，指定
- **reserve** 動 ①とっておく，備えておく ②～を予約する ③～を留保する
- **respect** 名 尊敬，尊重 動 ～を尊敬[尊重]する
- **responsibility** 名 ①責任，義務，義理 ②負担，責務
- **responsible** 形 責任のある，信頼できる，確実な
- **restroom** 名 (公共建物の)トイレ，休憩所
- **result** 名 結果，成り行き，成績 動 (結果として)起こる[生じる]，結局～になる
- **retail** 形 小売りの 名 小売り(店)
- **retailer** 名 小売業者，小売り商売をする人，小売店
- **retire** 動 引き下がる，退職[引退]する 形 《-d》退職[引退]した
- **return policy** 返品条件
- **revenue** 名 所得，収入，利益
- **revolve** 動 回転する[させる]，～

Word List

を中心に回る

- **ride** 名(遊園地などの)乗り物, (馬・乗り物に)乗ること 動~に乗る
- **right** 動正しい位置にする(戻す) 名権利
- **right away** すぐに
- **right-hand** 形右(側)の, 右手(用)の
- **ring** 名①輪, 円形, 指輪 ②競技場 動①~を輪でとり囲む ②鳴る[鳴らす] ③~に電話をかける
- **roast beef** ローストビーフ
- **roll** 動①ころがる[ころがす], うねる ②(時が)たつ 名一巻き
- **romance** 名恋愛(関係, 感情), 恋愛[空想, 冒険]小説
- **roof** 名屋根(のようなもの), 住居 動~に屋根をつける
- **roommate** 名ルームメイト, 部屋を共有する相手
- **root** 名①根, 根元 ②原因 ③《-s》先祖 動(熱狂的に)声援をおくる
- **rosy** 形バラのような, バラ色の, (顔色が健康的に)赤い
- **route** 名道, 道筋, 路線, ルート
- **row** 名(横に並んだ)列 **in a row** 1列に, 連続して 動①~を1列に並べる ②(舟)をこぐ
- **rural** 形田舎の, 地方の
- **rush** 動突進する, ~をせきたてる 名突進, 突撃, 殺到 形急ぎの, ラッシュの
- **Russian** 形ロシア人[語]の 名ロシア人[語]

S

- **safety** 名安全, 無事, 確実
- **sale** 名販売, 取引, 大売出し **sales clerk** 販売員, 店員
- **salespeople** 名販売員, 店員
- **sales tax** 売上税, 消費税
- **salon** 名①(美容関係の)店 ②客間, サロン
- **San Francisco** サンフランシスコ《地名》
- **Santa Claus** サンタクロース
- **sauce** 名ソース
- **savings account** 普通預金(口座)
- **scarves** 名scarf(スカーフ)の複数
- **screen** 名仕切り, 幕, スクリーン, 画面
- **search** 動(~を)捜し求める, 調べる 名捜査, 探索, 調査
- **security** 名安全性, 安心, 安全確保
- **security-check** 名安全確認
- **Seder** 名セダー《(ユダヤ人のエジプト脱出を記念する)過越祭りの儀式》
- **seem** 動~に見える, ~のように思われる
- **select** 動~を選択する 形選んだ, 一流の, えりぬきの
- **senior** 形年長の, 年上の, 古参の, 上級の 名年長者, 先輩, 先任者
- **sense** 名①感覚 ②《-s》正気, 本性 ③常識, 分別 ④意味 動~を感じる **make sense** 筋が通っている, なるほどと思える
- **sensitive** 形敏感な, 感度がいい, 繊細な, (問題などが)デリケートな
- **sentence** 名①文 ②判決, 宣告 動~に判決を下す, 宣告する
- **separate** 動分離[分割]する[させる], 別れる[別れさせる] 形分かれた, 別れた
- **series** 名一続き, シリーズ, 一組
- **serious** 形①まじめな, 真剣な ②重大な, 深刻な, (病気などが)重い
- **serve** 動①(~に)仕える, 奉仕する ②(客の)応対をする, (~に)給仕する ③(役目を)果たす, 勤める ④

GET TO KNOW THE USA: ENJOY YOUR VISIT

～を供する

- **service** 名①奉仕,貢献,サービス ②公共事業 ③兵役,軍務 動～の修理をする
- **set aside** 取っておく
- **set on** ～する気でいる,～するつもりである
- **settle** 動①安定する[させる], 落ち着く[落ち着かせる] ②(移り)住む, 定住する, 入植する
- **settler** 名移住者, 入植者
- **sex** 名性, 性別, 男女
- **shape** 名①形, 姿, 型 ②状態, 調子 動～を形作る, ～を具体化する
- **sharp** 形①鋭い, とがった ②刺すような, きつい ③鋭敏な 副①鋭く, 急に ②(時間が)ちょうど
- **shiver** 動(寒さなどで)身震いする[させる] 名悪寒
- **shopper** 名買い物客
- **short-term** 形短期間の
- **shoulder** 名肩 動①～を肩にかつぐ ②(責任などを)肩代わりする, 引き受ける
- **show off** 見せびらかす, よく見せる
- **show up** 姿を見せる, 来る
- **side** 名側, 横, そば, 斜面, 面 動味方する
- **sidewalk** 名歩道
- **sightseeing** 名観光, 見物
- **signal** 名信号, 合図, 信号機, 電波 動信号を送る, 合図する
- **silence** 名沈黙, 無言, 静寂 動～を沈黙させる, ～を静まらせる
- **similar** 形～に類似した
- **simply** 副①簡単に ②単に, ただ ③まったく
- **single** 形たった一つの, 独身の 名(ホテルなどの)1人用の部屋, シングルス[単試合]
- **situation** 名①場所, 位置 ②状況,

境遇, 立場

- **sixteenth** 名第16番目(の人[物]), 16日 形第16番目の
- **ski** 名スキー, スキー板
- **skill** 名①技能, 技術 ②上手, 熟練
- **slave** 名奴隷 動(奴隷のように)あくせく働く
- **slide** 動すべる[らせる], すべって行く, 滑走する 名すべること, 滑走, 滑走路, すべり台
- **slowly** 副遅く, ゆっくり
- **slowness** 名遅いこと, 緩慢
- **small talk** 世間話, おしゃべり
- **smelly** 形いやなにおいのする
- **smoke** 動喫煙する, 煙を出す 名①煙, 煙状のもの ②《-ing》喫煙 形《-ed》薫製にした
- **smoker** 名喫煙家, 煙草を吸う人
- **snack** 名軽食
- **snail** 名カタツムリ snail mail 従来の郵便
- **soap** 名石けん 動(～を)石けんで洗う
- **soccer** 名サッカー
- **social** 形①社会の, 社会的な ②社交的な, 愛想のよい social service 名社会事業, 社会福祉
- **socialize** 動社交的に交際する, つき合う
- **socially** 副社会的に, 社交的に
- **soda pop** 清涼飲料水
- **somebody** 代誰か, ある人
- **someone** 代ある人, 誰か
- **something** 代①ある物, 何か ②いくぶん, 多少
- **sometimes** 副ときどき
- **somewhere** 副①どこかへ[に] ②ある時, いつか, およそ
- **so on** その他もろもろ
- **sort** 名種類, 品質 動～を分類する

Word List

- **southern** 形 南の, 南向きの, 南からの
- **southwest** 名形 ①南西(の), 南西部(の) ②《S-》(米国の)南西部
- **souvenir** 名 おみやげ
- **Spanish** 形 スペイン[人(語)]の 名 スペイン語[人]
- **Spanish-speaking** 形 スペイン語を話す
- **speak out** はっきりと言う
- **specialness** 名 特別なこと, 独特なこと
- **specialty** 名 専門, 専攻, 本職, 得意 specialty store 専門店
- **specific** 形 明確な, はっきりした, 具体的な 名 細目
- **speed** 名 速力, 速度 動 急ぐ[急がせる]
- **spell** 動 ①(語)をつづる, 〜のつづりを言う ②〜を呪文にかける spell out スペリングを言う, 文字を略さずに書く 名 ③呪文, まじない
- **spirit** 名 ①霊 ②精神 ③蒸留酒
- **split** 動 裂く[ける], 割る[れる], 分裂させる[する] 裂くこと, 割れること, 裂け目, 割れ目
- **spot** 名 ①地点, 場所 ②斑点, しみ ③観光地, スポット 動 〜に点を打つ, 〜にしみをつける
- **sprang** 動 spring(跳ねる, 跳ぶ, 突然現れる)の過去
- **spread out** 広げ[が]る, 展開する
- **spring up** 急に起る, 突然現われる
- **spring break** 春休み
- **St. Patrick's Day** 聖パトリックデイ
- **stage** 名 ①舞台 ②段階 動 〜を上演する
- **stair** 名 ①(階段の)1段 ②《-s》階段, はしご

- **stamp** 名 ①印 ②切手 動 ①〜に印を押す ②〜を踏みつける
- **stand** 名 ①屋台, 売店 ②見物席
- **Staples** 名 ステイプルズ《米の文具販売チェーン》
- **state** 名 ①有様, 状態 ②《the -》国家, (アメリカなどの)州 動 〜を述べる 形 国家の state law 州法
- **stationery** 名 文房具
- **stay-at-home** 名 出不精(の人), 家にいる人 形 出不精の, 家にいたがる
- **steel** 名 鋼, 鋼鉄(製の物) 形 鋼鉄の, 堅い
- **step family** まま親のいる家庭
- **stereotype** 名 ステレオタイプ, 固定観念
- **stock** 名 ①貯蔵 ②仕入れ品, 在庫品 ③株式 動 仕入れる, 蓄える
- **stranger** 名 ①見知らぬ人, 他人 ②不案内[不慣れ]な人
- **street-smart** 形 世間慣れした
- **strengthen** 動 〜を強くする, しっかりさせる
- **strict** 形 厳しい, 厳密な
- **stroller** 名 ①放浪者 ②折りたたみ式の乳母車
- **struggle** 動 (〜しようと)もがく, 奮闘する 名 もがき, 奮闘
- **studio** 名 スタジオ, 仕事場, ワンルームマンション
- **stuff** 名 ①材料, 原料 ②もの 動 〜に詰める[詰め込む]
- **style** 名 やり方, 流儀, 様式, スタイル 動 〜と称する, 〜に称号を授ける
- **stylist** 名 スタイリスト
- **sublet** 名 また貸し(借り) 動 〜をまた貸し(借り)する
- **subletting** 名 また貸し, 下請け
- **subtle** 形 微妙な, かすかな, 繊細な, 敏感な, 器用な
- **suburb** 名 近郊, 郊外

GET TO KNOW THE USA: ENJOY YOUR VISIT

- **suburban** 形 郊外の, 郊外に住む
- **subway** 名 地下鉄, 地下道
- **succeed** 動 ①成功する ②(〜の)跡を継ぐ
- **success** 名 成功, 幸運, 上首尾
- **successful** 形 成功した, うまくいった
- **suffer** 動 損害を受ける, (病気に)なる, 苦しむ, 悩む
- **suit** 名 ①スーツ ②訴訟 動 適合する[させる], 似合う
- **suitcase** 名 スーツケース
- **Summer Time** サマータイム, 夏時間
- **supermarket** 名 スーパーマーケット
- **supersize** 動 超大型にする, サイズを非常に大きくする 形 非常に大きなサイズの
- **supply** 動 〜を供給[配給]する, 〜を補充する 名 供給(品), 給与, 補充
- **support** 動 ①〜を支える ②〜を養う, 〜を援助する 名 ①支え ②援助, 扶養
- **suppose** 動 〜と仮定する, 〜と推測する 《be -ed》〜と思われている **be supposed to do** 〜することになっている, 〜すべきである
- **surely** 副 確かに, きっと
- **surf** 動 ①波に乗る ②(インターネットで)情報を見る 名 打ち寄せる波 **surf's up** 波が割れていてサーフィンができる状態
- **surface** 名 表面, 水面 **surface mail** 船便
- **surround** 動 〜を囲む, 〜を包囲する
- **sweat** 名 汗 動 汗をかく
- **symbol** 名 シンボル, 象徴

T

- **tag** 名 札, 値札
- **tailgating** 名 直前の車にぴったりつけて運転すること
- **talented** 形 才能のある, 有能な
- **take leave** ①休みをとる ②いとまごいをする
- **take one's time** マイペースでいく, じっくりする
- **Target** 名 ターゲット《米のスーパーマーケットチェーン》
- **taste** 名 ①味, 風味 ②好み, 趣味 動 〜の味がする, (〜を)味わう
- **tasty** 形 おいしい
- **tax** 名 ①税 ②重荷, 重い負担 動 ①〜に課税する ②〜に重荷を負わせる
- **tax-deductible** 形 税控除の, 所得から控除できる
- **taxi** 名 タクシー
- **technology** 名 技術, テクノロジー
- **teenager** 名 十代, ティーンエイジャー
- **television** 名 テレビ
- **teller** 名 金銭出納係, 窓口
- **temperature** 名 温度, 体温
- **temple** 名 寺, 神殿
- **tend** 動 ①《- to》〜の傾向がある, 〜しがちである ②向かう, 行く
- **term** 名 ①期間, 期限 ②語, 言い方, 用語 ③条件
- **territory** 名 ①領土 ②(広い)地域, 範囲, 領域
- **terrorist** 名形 テロリスト(の)
- **Texas** 名 テキサス《地名》
- **text messages** テキストメッセージ, 携帯電話によるメール
- **text messaging** 文字によるメッセージ(米では携帯電話でのメールを指す)
- **TGI Friday's** TGIフライデーズ《米の外食チェーン店》

148

WORD LIST

- **Thanksgiving Day** 感謝祭, サンクス・ギビング・デー
- **theater** 名 劇場
- **therefore** 副 したがって, それゆえ, その結果
- **think up** 考えだす, 思いつく
- **though** 接 ①〜にもかかわらず, 〜だが ②たとえ〜でも 副 しかし
- **thus** 副 ①このように ②これだけ ③かくて, だから
- **tight** 形 堅い, きつい, ぴんと張った, 厳重な 副 堅く, しっかりと 《-s》タイツ
- **till** 前 〜まで 接 〜まで 動 (土地)を耕す
- **time-wise** 副 時間的には
- **time zone** 時間帯
- **tip** 名 ①チップ, 心づけ ②先端, 頂点 動 チップをやる
- **toast** 名 ①トースト ②乾杯 動 ①(パンなど)焼ける[焼く] ②火で暖まる[暖める] ③乾杯する
- **toe** 名 足指, つま先 **on one's toes** 元気な, 油断のない, 準備のできた
- **to go** 持ち帰り(用の)
- **toilet** 名 トイレ, 化粧室
- **token** 名 ①しるし ②トークン(地下鉄用のコイン)
- **toll-free** 形 通話料無料の, 料金のかからない
- **to name a few** 2, 3例をあげると
- **tool** 名 道具, 用具, 工具
- **torn** 動 tear (〜を裂く, 〜を引き離す)の過去分詞
- **total** 形 総計の, 全体の, 完全な 名 全体, 合計 動 〜を合計する
- **totally** 副 全体的に, すっかり
- **tour** 名 ツアー, 見て回ること, 視察
- **tourist** 名 旅行者
- **towel** 名 タオル

- **traffic** 名 通行, 往来, 交通(量), 貿易 **heavy traffic** 交通混雑 **traffic light** 信号 動 商売する, 取引する
- **transfer** 名 移動, 譲渡, 振替
- **translator** 名 翻訳者, 通訳者
- **transportation** 名 交通(機関), 輸送手段
- **treat** 動 ①〜を(取り)扱う ②〜を治療する ③おごる ④〜を(…と)みなす 名 楽しみ, もてなし
- **treatment** 名 取り扱い, 待遇
- **trend** 名 トレンド, 傾向
- **trendy** 形 流行の, 時代に合った
- **trick** 名 ①策略 ②いたずら, 冗談 ③手品, 錯覚 動 〜をだます **trick or treat**「お菓子をくれないといたずらするよ」
- **tricycle** 名 三輪車
- **truck** 名 トラック, 運搬車 動 〜をトラックで運ぶ
- **truly** 副 本当に, 心から
- **turkey** 名 七面鳥(の肉)
- **typewriter** 名 タイプライター

U

- **U.S.** 名 アメリカ合衆国 (=United States of America)
- **U.S. Census Bureau** 米国勢調査局
- **underground** 形 ①地下の[にある] ②地下組織の ③前衛的な 名 ①地下鉄, 地下(道) ②地下組織 ③前衛運動 副 地下に
- **undisciplined** 形 行儀の悪い, 訓練されていない
- **uneducated** 形 無教育な, 無学な
- **unfairness** 名 不公平, 不当
- **unfortunately** 副 不幸にも, 運悪く
- **unhappy** 形 不運な, 不幸な, 不満な

GET TO KNOW THE USA: ENJOY YOUR VISIT

- **unhealthy** 形健康でない
- **unique** 形唯一の, ユニークな, 独自の
- **unit** 名ユニット, 構成単位(一個, 一人)
- **United States (of America)** アメリカ合衆国
- **unknown** 形知られていない, 不明の
- **unless** 接もし〜でなければ, 〜しなければ
- **unlike** 形似ていない, 違った 前〜とは違って
- **unlucky** 形①不運な ②不吉な, 縁起の悪い
- **unnecessary** 形不必要な, 余分な, 必要以上の
- **unpleasant** 形不愉快な, 気にさわる, いやな, 不快な
- **unusual** 形普通でない, 珍しい, 見[聞き]慣れない
- **upon** 前①《場所・接触》〜(の上)に ②《日・時》〜に ③《関係・従事》〜に関して, 〜について 副前へ, 続けて
- **urban** 形都会の, 都会ふうの
- **used to** ①(以前は)よく〜したものだった ②《be-》〜に慣れている
- **usual** 形通常の, いつもの, 平常の, ふつうの 名おきまりのこと

V

- **vaccine** 名ワクチン
- **Valentine's Day** バレンタイン・デイ
- **valuable** 形貴重な, 価値のある, 役に立つ
- **value** 名価値, 値打ち, 価格 動〜を評価する, 〜に値をつける
- **Van Gogh** ヴァン・ゴッホ《画家》
- **variety** 名①変化, 多様性, 寄せ集め ②種類
- **various** 形変化に富んだ, さまざまの, たくさんの
- **vary** 動変わる[変える], 〜を変更する, 異なる
- **vegetable** 名野菜, 青物 形野菜の, 植物(性)の
- **vendor** 名売る人, 露天の物売り
- **versus** 前対, 〜に対して
- **Veterans Day** 復員軍人の日
- **Vietnamese** 名形ベトナム(の), ベトナム人[語](の)
- **viewer** 名視聴者, 観察者
- **visible** 形目に見える, 明らかな
- **visitor** 名訪問客
- **voice-mail** 名音声によるメッセージ, 留守番電話

W

- **waiter** 名ウエイター, 給仕
- **Wal-Mart** 名ウォルマート《米のスーパーマーケットチェーン》
- **warehouse** 名倉庫, 問屋, 商品保管所
- **Washington D.C.** ワシントンD.C.《地名》
- **Washington's Birthday** ワシントン大統領誕生記念日
- **WASP** 略ワスプ(アングロサクソン系白人新教徒=White Anglo-Saxon Protestant)
- **weather-wise** 副天気に関していえば, 天気の点では
- **web** 名①クモの巣 ②《the W-》ウェブ(World Wide Web)
- **wedding** 名結婚式, 婚礼
- **weekday** 名週日, 平日 形平日の
- **weekly** 形週に1度の, 毎週の 名週刊誌

WORD LIST

- **weighing** 形 重さがある
- **weight** 名 ①重さ, 重力 ②重荷, 負担 ③重大さ, 勢力 動 ①~に重みをつける ②~に重荷を負わせる
- **well-developed** 形 よく開発された, よく発達した
- **well-known** 形 よく知られた, 有名な
- **West Coast** 西海岸《米の太平洋岸地域》
- **whatever** 代 ①~するものは何でも ②どんなこと[もの]~とも 形 ①どんな~でも ②《否定文, 疑問文で》少しの~も, 何らかの
- **wheelchair** 名 車いす
- **whenever** 接 ①~するときはいつでも, ~するたびに ②いつ~しても 副 一体いつ
- **wherever** 接 どこでも, どこへ[で]~するとも 副 一体どこへ[に, で]
- **whether** 接 ~かどうか, ~かまたは…, ~であろうとなかろうと
- **White Pages** 個人別の電話帳
- **whole** 形 全体の, すべての, 完全な, 満~, 丸~ 名《the-》全体, 全部
- **wholesale** 名 卸売り 形 卸の, 大規模な
- **wide** 形 幅の広い, 広範囲の 副 広く, 大きく開いて
- **widely** 副 広く, 広範囲にわたって
- **will** 名 意志, 願望 ②遺言, 遺書
- **willingness** 名 意欲, 快く~すること
- **winner** 名 勝利者, 成功者
- **win over** 説得する, 味方に引き入れる
- **winter break** 冬休み
- **wise** 形 賢明な, 聡明な, 博学の
- **within** 前 ①~の中[内]に, ~の内部に ②~以内で, ~を越えないで 副 中[内]へ[に], 内部に 名 内部

- **wives** 名 wife (妻, 夫人)の複数
- **wonder** 動 ①不思議に思う, (~に)驚く ②~かしら(と思う) 名 驚き(の念), 不思議なもの **no wonder** 驚くに値しない
- **worker** 名 働く人, 労働者
- **workplace** 名 職場, 仕事場
- **World Series** ワールドシリーズ《野球》
- **World War I** 第一次世界大戦《1914–18》
- **World War II** 第二次世界大戦《1939–45》
- **worn** 形 すり切れた, 使い古しの 動 wear (~を着ている, 疲れる, 消耗する)の過去, 過去分詞
- **worse** 形 いっそう悪い, より劣った, よりひどい 副 いっそう悪く
- **worth** 形 ~の価値がある, ~しがいがある 名 価値, 値打ち
- **wrapper** 名 包装紙, 包装係

Y

- **yearend** 名 年度末
- **Yellow Pages** 職業別電話帳

Z

- **ZIP** 名 郵便番号
- **zone** 名 地帯, 区域

E-CAT

English **C**onversational **A**bility **T**est
国際英語会話能力検定

● E-CATとは…
英語が話せるようになるための
テストです。インターネット
ベースで、30分であなたの発
話力をチェックします。

www.ecatexam.com

iTEP

● iTEP®とは…
世界各国の企業、政府機関、アメリカの大学
300校以上が、英語能力判定テストとして採用。
オンラインによる90分のテストで文法、リー
ディング、リスニング、ライティング、スピー
キングの5技能をスコア化。iTEP®は、留学、就
職、海外赴任などに必要な、世界に通用する英
語力を総合的に評価する画期的なテストです。

www.itepexamjapan.com

ラダーシリーズ
Get to Know the USA *Vol.1*
Enjoy Your Visit アメリカに行こう

2005年 9月10日　第 1 刷発行
2022年 5月 8日　第12刷発行

著　者　黒田　基子

発行者　浦　　晋亮

発行所　IBCパブリッシング株式会社
　　　　〒162-0804 東京都新宿区中里町29番3号
　　　　菱秀神楽坂ビル
　　　　Tel. 03-3513-4511　Fax. 03-3513-4512
　　　　www.ibcpub.co.jp

© Motoko Kuroda 2005
© IBC Publishing, Inc. 2005

印刷　株式会社シナノパブリッシングプレス
装丁　伊藤 理恵
組版データ　New Aster Medium+ Minion Pro Bold + Lucida Sans Demibold

落丁本・乱丁本は、小社宛にお送りください。送料小社負担にてお取り替えいたし
ます。本書の無断複写 (コピー) は著作権法上での例外を除き禁じられています。

Printed in Japan
ISBN978-4-89684-035-3